Register Your Book

Register your copy of "The ASCA National Model: A Framework for School Counseling Programs (third edition)" to get these benefits:

- Electronic copies of all templates for you to use in building your own program
- Discounted pricing on the digital and app version of the ASCA National Model, which contains enhanced content, training videos, electronic templates and more
- Opportunity to be among the first to learn about enhancements to the digital edition and app

To register your book, visit *www.ASCANationalModel.org/register* and input the serial number found in the lower right-hand corner of this page to begin taking advantage of your additional benefits.

71407418

ASCA National Model

A Framework for School Counseling Programs

THIRD EDITION

AMERICAN
SCHOOL
COUNSELOR
ASSOCIATION

ONE VISION ONE VOICE

Citation Guide

When citing from this publication, use the following reference:

American School Counselor Association (2012). The ASCA National Model: A Framework for School Counseling Programs, Third Edition. Alexandria, VA: Author.

The American School Counselor Association (ASCA) supports school counselors' efforts to help students focus on academic, personal/social and career development so they achieve success in school and are prepared to lead fulfilling lives as responsible members of society. ASCA, which is the school counseling division of the American Counseling Association, provides professional development, publications and other resources, research and advocacy to professional school counselors around the globe. For more information, visit *www.schoolcounselor.org*.

1101 King St., Suite 625, Alexandria, VA 22314

(703) 683-ASCA, (800) 306-4722, fax: (703) 683-1619
www.schoolcounselor.org
ISBN 978-1-929289-32-5

Table of Contents

III. Management

IV. Delivery

V. Accountability

The ASCA National Model diamond graphic is a registered trademark of the American School Counselor Association and may not be reprinted or modified without permission.

Preface

EMBRACE THE PAST, WELCOME THE FUTURE:
A BRIEF HISTORY OF SCHOOL COUNSELING

By Norman C. Gysbers, Ph.D., Curators' Professor, University of Missouri – Columbia

School counseling is 100-plus years old. It evolved shaped by various economic, social and educational forces guided by the work of many individuals. The ASCA National Model, first published in 2003 and now in its third edition, is a product of this evolution. By embracing knowledge from the past, we can learn how school counseling evolved from a position, to a service, to a program, the organizational concept embedded in the ASCA National Model. By welcoming the future we can combine the insights gained from the past with new knowledge, enabling us to continue to develop and fully implement comprehensive school counseling programs in every school district in the country.

School counseling as we know it today began as vocational guidance in the early 1900s. It was established in schools as a position occupied by administrators and teachers. No organizational structure was provided other than a list of duties. In the 1920s school counseling began to change, shaped by the mental hygiene, psychometric and child study movements. As a result, a more clinically oriented approach to school counseling emerged. This signaled a shift away from economic issues to psychological issues with an emphasis on counseling for personal adjustment.

During the 1930s, discussion took place concerning the various personnel responsible for school counseling, the duties they performed, and their selection and training. A major milestone occurred with the creation of a new organizational structure called pupil personnel services. Within that structure, the concept of guidance services emerged. The field of school counseling had moved from a position with a list of duties to a position with a list of duties organized by guidance services all under the overall structure of pupil personnel services.

The 1940s and 1950s saw the expansion and extension of counseling in the schools. The literature during years 1941–1945 focused on contributions to the war effort. After 1945, attention returned to the need for counseling in the schools and on ways to improve the services provided. The selection and training of school counselors also received attention and support with the passage of the Vocational Education Act of 1946 and the National Defense Education Act (NDEA) of 1958. In addition, the American School Counselor Association was established in 1952 as a division of the American Personnel and Guidance Association. Now school counselors had a national organization and a voice in national affairs.

A major issue being debated in the 1960s and 1970s concerned the nature of school counseling. Was it more psychological in nature featuring counseling as a major intervention? Was it more educational in nature featuring a broader array of interventions including counseling but also information, assessment, placement and follow-up activities? Although school counseling at the elementary level had been discussed previously, it wasn't until the 1960s that it became a reality. NDEA, amended in the 1960s, stimulated training practices and procedures that set elementary school counseling apart from secondary school counseling. The 1960s and 1970s also witnessed increasing concern about the services model of school counseling. Calls for change came from a variety of sources ending up in the beginning development of a comprehensive program approach to school counseling.

The concept of a program for school counseling began to take form in the 1960s and 1970s and then became a major way to organize and manage school counseling in the schools in the 1980s, 1990s and into the 21st century. During this time many states developed state models. Training programs to help personnel in school districts plan, design and implement comprehensive school counseling programs also were initiated.

The role and functions of school counselors was of concern during the 1980s and 1990s. Some writers advocated the role of human development specialist; others recommended the role of change agent. Predominating roles were coordinating, counseling and consulting. Tied to the role and function issue was the issue of terminology. Is it guidance, guidance and counseling or school counseling?

Although progress was made in developing, implementing and evaluating comprehensive school counseling programs in the first decade of the 21st century, discussion continued about program purposes and the work of school counselors. Should the focus be educational (academic), vocational (career) or personal/social (mental health)? Some writers focused on academic achievement and career but not personal/social or mental health. Other writers urged the opposite with mental health issues needing more attention. Still other writers urged the adoption of a holistic approach emphasizing attention to all three areas.

During this same decade discussion about program purposes and school counselors' roles continued with some writers emphasizing an advocacy change agent focus. Others talked about the need to emphasize collaboration. Still others recommended school counselors do more indirect work and less direct work with students. Finally there was a movement for school counselors to become more data-oriented, using data to identify school concerns and student needs.

The development and implementation of school counseling programs across the country grew in the first decade of the 21st century. This growth was stimulated by the publication of the ASCA National Model in 2003 and its adoption by many states and school districts. A second edition was published in 2005.

As the second decade of the 21st century began, an ongoing issue for school counseling was accountability. Although this has been part of professional discussion since the 1920s, and much work was done over the ensuing years, there is a renewed sense of urgency today concerning accountability. The literature makes it clear that evaluation is here to stay and needs to be designed and carried out to not only demonstrate effectiveness but also to improve the work of school counselors.

What will the next 100 years be like? No one knows for sure, but if the next 100 years are like the first 100 years, school counseling will continue to evolve. The forces that shaped school counseling so far will continue to do so, and discussion about purposes and organization will continue. So, while no one knows what the future holds, current literature suggests that at least for the near future students and their parents in school districts across the country will continue to benefit from having fully implemented school counseling programs. Embrace the past, welcome the future.

This article was adapted from material in Gysbers, N. C. (2010), *Remembering the Past, Shaping the Future: A History of School Counseling*. Alexandria, VA: American School Counselor Association.

Introduction

This third edition of "The ASCA National Model: A Framework for School Counseling Programs" is a logical progression in the journey of the school counseling profession. As Norm Gysbers describes, the history of school counseling has been fraught with many twists and turns, leaving a trail littered with artifacts of each change of direction. As a result, the role of school counselors and school counseling had not been clearly understood among school staff, administrators, parents and even among school counselors themselves. Consequently, school counseling differed enormously from state to state, district to district and even school to school. The effectiveness of school counseling also was inconsistent.

In 2001, ASCA initiated efforts to reconcile all the developments in the profession during the previous 100 years. A group of theorists, practitioners and other school counseling experts was convened to help the profession progress along its path. The group agreed that a model was needed to help all school counselors become valuable contributors to the accomplishment of their school mission.

Two years later, in 2003, the first edition of the ASCA National Model was published to serve several purposes.

- The ASCA National Model helped move school counseling from a responsive service provided for some students to a program for every student. School counseling programs don't address just the highest or lowest performing students or those experiencing a crisis or other need at a given time. The ASCA National Model reinforced the idea that school counselors help every student improve academic achievement, navigate personal and social development and plan for successful careers after graduation.
- The ASCA National Model provided uniformity to standardize school counseling programs across the country. Although flexibility is built in to allow school counselors to customize the program to meet the individual needs of their students, the ASCA National Model provides a framework of components that all school counseling programs should exhibit.

- The ASCA National Model helped to re-establish school counseling as a crucial educational function that is integral to academic achievement and overall student success. The objective of school counseling is to help students overcome barriers to learning.

The ASCA National Model also required school counselors to think in terms of new paradigms. School counseling programs need to be comprehensive in scope, results-oriented in design and developmental in nature. The transition from service to program necessitated that school counselors become leaders to manage the program. To do this, school counselors could no longer operate in isolation. They need to collaborate with other school staff, parents, community resources and students. Because school counseling cuts across all curricular areas, school counselors often are the only adults who have a big picture of the students; therefore school counselors need to advocate for their students to allow students to become successful. That advocacy and other work of school counselors should lead to changes in the school culture to create the optimal environment for learning.

Since the ASCA National Model was first introduced, ASCA staff has received thousands of comments, many suggesting changes that could clarify some confusion in language and help it become easier to read and implement. Staff compiled the changes into a revised draft, which was sent to an advisory committee of practicing school counselors and professors of school counseling, including Trish Hatch and Judy Bowers, authors of the original ASCA National Model. Comments from the advisory committee were incorporated into a revised draft, which was posted for public comment. Changes suggested through the public comments were used to develop this third edition.

Some of the major changes from the previous edition include expanded sections about the four themes of leadership, advocacy, collaboration and systemic change. There also are special topics that discuss various components of the ASCA National Model in greater detail. Most importantly, much of the language has been clarified, and in some cases, sections have been moved, to make the ASCA National Model easier to read, understand and implement. A full explanation of the changes is presented as Appendix A. In addition, the digital edition and app have created opportunities for interactive tools that will make implementation easier and in real time, no matter where programs, interactions and activities occur – at your desk, in the hallway, out in the school or even at district or community events.

Shortly after ASCA introduced the ASCA National Model, ASCA initiated the Recognized ASCA Model Program (RAMP) designation, which highlights school counseling programs that have demonstrated advanced implementation of comprehensive, results-based, developmental programs. School counselors at schools that have received the RAMP designation say the designation not only was a great honor but the process helped them improve their program even more.

The school counseling profession has made tremendous strides since the ASCA National Model was first introduced. This third edition and subsequent editions are intended to carry school counselors and school counseling farther along their journey and ever closer to their goal of helping every student succeed.

Kwok-Sze Wong, Ed.D., ASCA Executive Director

Executive Summary

School counselors design and deliver comprehensive school counseling programs that promote student achievement. These programs are comprehensive in scope, preventive in design and developmental in nature. "The ASCA National Model: A Framework for School Counseling Programs" outlines the components of a comprehensive school counseling program. The ASCA National Model brings school counselors together with one vision and one voice, which creates unity and focus toward improving student achievement.

A comprehensive school counseling program is an integral component of the school's academic mission. Comprehensive school counseling programs, driven by student data and based on standards in academic, career and personal/social development, promote and enhance the learning process for all students. The ASCA National Model:
- ensures equitable access to a rigorous education for all students
- identifies the knowledge and skills all students will acquire as a result of the K-12 comprehensive school counseling program
- is delivered to all students in a systematic fashion
- is based on data-driven decision making
- is provided by a state-credentialed school counselor

Effective school counseling programs are a collaborative effort between the school counselor, parents and other educators to create an environment that promotes student achievement. Staff and school counselors value and respond to the diversity and individual differences in our societies and communities. Comprehensive school counseling programs ensure equitable access to opportunities and rigorous curriculum for all students to participate fully in the educational process.

School counselors focus their skills, time and energy on direct and indirect services to students. To achieve maximum program effectiveness, the American School Counselor Association recommends a school counselor to student ratio of 1:250 and that school counselors spend 80 percent or more of their time in direct and indirect services to students. School counselors participate as members of the educational team and use the skills of leadership, advocacy and collaboration to promote systemic change as appropriate. The framework of a comprehensive school counseling program consists of four components: foundation, management, delivery and accountability.

FOUNDATION

School counselors create comprehensive school counseling programs that focus on student outcomes, teach student competencies and are delivered with identified professional competencies.

Program Focus: To establish program focus, school counselors identify personal beliefs that address how all students benefit from the school counseling program. Building on these beliefs, school counselors create a vision statement defining what the future will look like in terms of student outcomes. In addition, school counselors create a mission statement aligned with their school's mission and develop program goals defining how the vision and mission will be measured.

Student Competencies: Enhancing the learning process for all students, the ASCA Student Standards guide the development of effective school counseling programs around three domains: academic, career and personal/social development. School counselors also consider how other student standards important to state and district initiatives complement and inform their school counseling program.

Professional Competencies: The ASCA School Counselor Competencies outline the knowledge, attitudes and skills that ensure school counselors are equipped to meet the rigorous demands of the profession. The ASCA Ethical Standards for School Counselors specify the principles of ethical behavior necessary to maintain the highest standard of integrity, leadership and professionalism. They guide school counselors' decision-making and help to standardize professional practice to protect both students and school counselors.

MANAGEMENT

School counselors incorporate organizational assessments and tools that are concrete, clearly delineated and reflective of the school's needs. Assessments and tools include:
- **School counselor competency and school counseling program assessments** to self-evaluate areas of strength and improvement for individual skills and program activities
- **Use-of-time assessment** to determine the amount of time spent toward the recommended 80 percent or more of the school counselor's time to direct and indirect services with students
- **Annual agreements** developed with and approved by administrators at the beginning of the school year addressing how the school counseling program is organized and what goals will be accomplished
- **Advisory councils** made up of students, parents, teachers, school counselors, administrators and community members to review and make recommendations about school counseling program activities and results

- **Use of data** to measure the results of the program as well as to promote systemic change within the school system so every student graduates college- and career-ready
- **Curriculum, small-group and closing-the-gap action plans** including developmental, prevention and intervention activities and services that measure the desired student competencies and the impact on achievement, behavior and attendance
- **Annual and weekly calendars** to keep students, parents, teachers and administrators informed and to encourage active participation in the school counseling program

DELIVERY

School counselors provide services to students, parents, school staff and the community in the following areas:

Direct Student Services

Direct services are in-person interactions between school counselors and students and include the following:

- **School counseling core curriculum:** This curriculum consists of structured lessons designed to help students attain the desired competencies and to provide all students with the knowledge, attitudes and skills appropriate for their developmental level. The school counseling core curriculum is delivered throughout the school's overall curriculum and is systematically presented by school counselors in collaboration with other professional educators in K-12 classroom and group activities.
- **Individual student planning:** School counselors coordinate ongoing systemic activities designed to assist students in establishing personal goals and developing future plans.
- **Responsive services:** Responsive services are activities designed to meet students' immediate needs and concerns. Responsive services may include counseling in individual or small-group settings or crisis response.

Indirect Student Services

Indirect services are provided on behalf of students as a result of the school counselors' interactions with others including referrals for additional assistance, consultation and collaboration with parents, teachers, other educators and community organizations.

ACCOUNTABILITY

To demonstrate the effectiveness of the school counseling program in measurable terms, school counselors analyze school and school counseling program data to determine how students are different as a result of the school counseling program. School counselors use data to show the impact of the school counseling program on student achievement, attendance and behavior and analyze school counseling program assessments to guide future action and improve future results for all students. The performance of the school counselor is evaluated on basic standards of practice expected of school counselors implementing a comprehensive school counseling program.

The ASCA National Model Themes

ASCA incorporates the four themes of leadership, advocacy, collaboration and systemic change as part of the framework of the ASCA National Model (The Education Trust, 1997). In the ASCA National Model graphic, the four themes are repeated around the frame to indicate the importance of school counselors' work within these areas (see page vi). School counselors play a significant part in improving student achievement and are uniquely positioned to be student and systems advocates. Through application of leadership, advocacy and collaboration skills as a part of a comprehensive school counseling program, school counselors promote student achievement and systemic change that ensures equity and access to rigorous education for every student and leads to closing achievement, opportunity and attainment gaps (Dahir & Stone, 2009; Martin & House, 2002).

LEADERSHIP

From providing leadership for the development of a comprehensive school counseling program to solving problems with school and community groups that promote student achievement, school counselors are called to be leaders in a variety of ways.

School counseling leadership:
- supports academic achievement and student development
- advances effective delivery of the comprehensive school counseling program
- promotes professional identity
- overcomes challenges of role inconsistency (Shillingford & Lambie, 2010)

Leadership is an essential skill for school counselors as they develop and manage a comprehensive school counseling program. As the other themes of advocacy, collaboration and systemic change require leadership to some degree, leadership may be the foundation of the other essential skills needed for program implementation (Mason & McMahon, 2009).

Leadership has been defined in many ways, such as:

Leadership is a process whereby an individual influences a group of individuals to achieve a common goal (Northouse, 2007).

and

The essence of leadership is not commanding, but teaching. It is opening people's eyes and minds. It is teaching them new ways to see the world and pointing them to new goals. It is giving them the motivation and discipline to achieve those goals. And it is teaching them to share their own knowledge and teach others. (Tichy, 2004)

Regardless of what definition of leadership is used, the design, development and implementation of a comprehensive school counseling program aligned with the ASCA National Model requires school counselors to understand and utilize leadership skills. School counselors can implement a program addressing the academic, career and personal/social needs of all students through the use of leadership practices (Mason, 2010).

After examining effective leadership, Bolman and Deal (2008) identified four leadership situations or contexts: structural, human resource, political and symbolic. When the leadership contexts are applied to comprehensive school counseling programs, school counselors can demonstrate specific activities that demonstrate each of these contexts of leadership through implementation of a comprehensive school counseling program.

The following chart shows examples of how activities within the ASCA National Model promote effective leadership as presented through the lens of four leadership contexts and research in school counseling leadership activities (Dollarhide, 2003).

Leadership Context (Bolman & Deal, 1997/2008)	School Counseling Leadership Activities (Dollarhide, 2003)	Leadership Components of the ASCA National Model
Structural leadership: Leadership in the building of viable organizations	1. Build the foundation of an effective school counseling program. 2. Attain technical mastery of counseling and education. 3. Design strategies for growth of the school counseling program. 4. Implement an effective school counseling program.	1. Define program focus, select appropriate student competencies, and adhere to professional competencies. 2. Analyze results of school counselor competency assessment to inform areas of growth for professional development. 3. Analyze results of school counseling program assessment and design strategies to continue to improve the comprehensive school counseling program. 4. Analyze program results. (curriculum, small-group and closing-the-gap results reports), and consider implications about program effectiveness.

Leadership Context (Bolman & Deal, 1997/2008)	School Counseling Leadership Activities (Dollarhide, 2003)	Leadership Components of the ASCA National Model
Human resource leadership: Leadership via empowerment and inspiration of followers	1. Believe in people.	1. Discuss and define beliefs about the ability of all students to achieve, including how, with parents, staff and community support.
	2. Communicate that belief.	2. Publicize vision statement focusing on the preferred future where school counseling goals and strategies are being successfully achieved. Publicize mission statement providing the focus and direction to reach the vision. Publicize program goals defining how the mission and vision will be accomplished.
	3. Be visible and accessible.	3. Publicize annual and weekly calendars with detailed information about school counseling core curriculum, individual student planning, responsive services and collaboration with parents, staff and community.
	4. Empower others.	4. Provide instruction to students to ensure development of competencies promoting the knowledge, attitudes and skills needed for student achievement, success and development.
Political leadership: Leadership in the use of interpersonal and organizational power	1. Understand the distribution of power within the building and district.	1. Present annual agreement to principal each year, including a formal discussion of the alignment of school and school counseling program mission and goals and detailing specific school counselor responsibilities.
	2. Build linkages with important stakeholders (e.g., parents, administrators, teachers, board members).	2. Participate on school and district committees to advocate for student programs and resources. Establish advisory council including representatives of key stakeholders selected to review and advise on the implementation of the school counseling program. Team and partner with staff, parents, businesses and community organizations to support student achievement for all students.
	3. Use persuasion and negotiation.	3. Advocate for student support, equity and access to a rigorous education with education stakeholders.

Leadership Context (Bolman & Deal, 1997/2008)	School Counseling Leadership Activities (Dollarhide, 2003)	Leadership Components of the ASCA National Model
Symbolic leadership: Leadership via the interpretation and re-interpretation of the meaning of change	1. Use symbols and metaphors to gain attention of followers. 2. Frame experience in meaningful ways for followers. 3. Discover and communicate a vision. 4. Maintain a relationship with the community you represent (e.g., students, parents, school colleagues). 5. Model health on all levels to inspire others. 6. Lead by example.	1. Present school profile data and program results data (process, perception and outcome) to promote awareness of student needs and program outcomes. 2. Organize program lessons and activities aligned with student needs, and promote student achievement for all students. 3. Publicize vision statement focusing on the preferred future where school counseling goals and strategies are being successfully achieved. 4. Provide direct services to all students; collaborate and communicate with parents, teachers, administrators and staff to promote a positive school climate and student achievement. 5. Follow ASCA Ethical Standards for School Counselors to demonstrate high standards of integrity, leadership and professionalism. 6. Regularly evaluate the school counseling program to determine its effectiveness and to identify areas of strength and areas for growth.

ADVOCACY

As educational leaders, school counselors are ideally situated to serve as advocates for every student in meeting high academic, career and personal/social standards. Advocating for the academic achievement of every student is a key role of school counselors and places them at the forefront of efforts to promote school reform.

To promote student achievement, school counselors advocate for students' academic, career and personal/social development needs and work to ensure these needs are addressed throughout the K-12 school experience. School counselors believe, support and promote every student's opportunity to achieve success in school.

The following table shows how school counselors demonstrate advocacy through specific topics from the ASCA National Model. Using the American Counseling Association's Advocacy Competencies (2003) as a conceptualization of advocacy, the topics of the ASCA National Model are provided as examples of how school counselors can advocate for students, from the micro-level to the macro-level, through the school counseling program.

	ACA Advocacy Competencies	Advocacy Components of the ASCA National Model
	Acting With Students	**Direct Student Services**

	Student Empowerment – Efforts that facilitate the identification of external barriers and development of self-advocacy skills, strategies and resources in response to those barriers.	1. School counseling core curriculum
		  ▪ Instruction
		  ▪ Group activities
		2. Individual student planning
		  ▪ Appraisal
		  ▪ Advisement
		3. Responsive services
		  ▪ Counseling (individual/small group)
		  ▪ Crisis response

	Acting on Behalf of Students	**Indirect Student Services and Program Management**
Micro-level	**Student Advocacy –** Assessing the need for direct intervention within the system on behalf of the student, identifying allies and carrying out a plan of action	▪ Referrals ▪ Consultation ▪ Collaboration ▪ School data profile ▪ Closing-the-gap and small-group action plans
	School/Community Collaboration – Actions where the school counselor and community collaborate to address a problem and devise an advocacy plan	▪ Advisory council ▪ Program goals ▪ Curriculum action plan
	Systems Advocacy – Identifying systemic problem, gaining information and insight from those who are most affected and implementing advocacy at a systems level	▪ Consultation ▪ Collaboration ▪ Annual agreement ▪ School data profile analysis ▪ Needs assessments ▪ Action plans ▪ Results reports analysis ▪ Program assessment analysis ▪ Program goal analysis

DATA DRIVEN

	ACA Advocacy Competencies	Advocacy Components of the ASCA National Model
	Acting on Behalf of Students	**Indirect Student Services and Program Management**
Macro-level	**Public Information** – Collaboration between school counselor and community in efforts to alert the public to macro-level issues regarding human dignity	▪ Collaboration with community groups ▪ Beliefs ▪ Vision statement ▪ Mission statement ▪ Advisory council ▪ Results reports ▪ School committees ▪ Sharing results
	Social/Political Advocacy – Recognizing when student problems must be addressed at a policy or legislative level and advocating for change within those areas	▪ District committees ▪ Board presentations ▪ Involvement with state and national professional associations ▪ Legislative interactions
	Adapted from Lewis, Arnold, House & Toporek (2003) and Toporek, Lewis & Crethar, (2009)	Adapted from Ratts, DeKruyf, & Chen-Hayes (2007)

COLLABORATION

School counselors work with stakeholders, both inside and outside the school, as a part of the comprehensive school counseling program. Through school, family and community collaboration, school counselors can access a vast array of support for student achievement and development that cannot be achieved by an individual, or school, alone.

School counselors collaborate in many ways. Within the school, school counselors build effective teams by encouraging collaboration among students, teachers, administrators and school staff to work toward the common goals of equity, access and academic success for every student. Outside of school, school counselors create effective working relationships with parents, community members and community agencies, tapping into resources that may not be available at the school. By understanding and appreciating the contributions made by others in educating all children, school counselors build a sense of community, which serves as a platform to create an environment encouraging success for every student.

Lawson (2003) identified 10 varieties of collaboration, seven of which relate specifically to the role of the school counselor.

▪ Interprofessional collaboration: includes school counselors, teachers, administrators, social workers, psychologists, nurses and other helping professionals who comprise sustainable teams.

- Youth-centered collaboration: viewing youth as experts and partners who share responsibility and accountability for results.

- Parent-centered collaboration: viewing parents as experts and partners, sharing accountability for results and whose engagement and well-being influence and determine their children's well-being.

- Family-centered collaboration: viewing family systems as partners sharing accountability for results and whose engagement influences and determines the well-being of children, parents and grandparents as well as the future of the family.

- Intra-organizational collaboration: includes people in the same organization, such as collaboration among school professionals, secretaries, custodians, cafeteria workers, bus drivers and community leaders, who may serve on site-based teams.

- Inter-organizational collaboration: includes groups of organizations such as community agencies, faith-based organizations, social service agencies and health clinics.

- Community collaboration: secures the engagement, mutual accountability and co-production capacities of all of the legitimate stakeholders in a workable geographic area.

The relationship among collaborators is a critical element for effective collaboration. A collaborative report on school principal/school counselor relationship identified characteristics of an effective relationship, and these characteristics can be applied to any collaborative relationship. The following table shows components of the ASCA National Model that promote relationships for effective collaboration.

Characteristics of Effective Relationships	Collaborative Components of the ASCA National Model
Open communication providing multiple opportunities for input to decision making	▪ Advisory council ▪ Use of data ▪ Needs assessments
Opportunities to share ideas on teaching, learning and schoolwide educational initiatives	▪ Teaming and partnering ▪ School/district committees
Sharing information about needs within the school and the community	▪ School data profile analysis ▪ Sharing program results
School counselor participation on school leadership teams	▪ Teaming and partnering ▪ School/district committees
Joint responsibility in the development of goals and metrics indicating success	▪ Program goals ▪ Annual agreement ▪ Action plans ▪ Results reports

Characteristics of Effective Relationships	Collaborative Components of the ASCA National Model
Joint responsibility in the development of goals and metrics indicating success	▪ Program goals ▪ Annual agreement ▪ Action plans ▪ Results reports
A shared vision of what is meant by student success	▪ Beliefs ▪ Vision statement ▪ Mission statement ▪ Program goals
Shared decision making on initiatives affecting student success	▪ Program goals ▪ Annual agreement
A collective commitment to equity and opportunity	▪ Beliefs ▪ Vision statement ▪ Mission statement ▪ Program goals ▪ Closing-the-gap results reports ▪ Leadership ▪ Advocacy ▪ Systemic Change

Adapted from *Finding a Way: Practical Examples of How an Effective Principal-Counselor Relationship Can Lead to Success for All Students* (2009).

SYSTEMIC CHANGE

Schools are a system, just like a family is a system. When an event occurs that makes an impact on one member of the family or part of the system, it affects other, if not all other, parts of the system. Comprehensive school counseling programs are an important part of the school's system, and through careful, data-driven implementation, an ASCA National Model program can have a positive impact on many other parts of the school's system that lead to student achievement and overall success.

With the expectation to serve the needs of every student, school counselors are uniquely positioned to identify systemic barriers to student achievement. School counselors have access to schoolwide achievement, attendance and behavioral data that not only informs the school counseling program but often underscores the need to identify and remove barriers that prevent all students from achieving college and career readiness. School counselors use these data to support leadership, advocacy and collaboration designed to create systemic change.

Systemic barriers may exist on any level, ranging from state or federal law, to district policies, to school and classroom procedures. These barriers are often identified after a review of data reveals gaps between student groups in achievement, opportunities and attainment. Through implementation of a comprehensive school counseling program, school counselors work proactively with students, parents, teachers, administrators and the community to remove systemic barriers to learning and to promote systemic change that will create a learning environment where all students succeed.

Systemic change does not occur overnight. But one small change can lead to another, which can lead to even larger and more impactful changes in the future. The following describes six stages of systemic change based on experiences in systemic change from across the United States and at all levels of education (Anderson, 1994).

Maintenance of the old system: Educators focus on maintaining the system as originally designed. They do not recognize that the system is fundamentally out of sync with the conditions of today's world. New knowledge about teaching, learning and organizational structures has not been incorporated into the present structure.

Awareness: Multiple stakeholders become aware that the current system is not working as well as it should, but they are unclear about what is needed instead.

Exploration: Educators and policymakers study and visit places that are trying new approaches. They try new ways of teaching and managing, generally in low-risk situations.

Transition: The scales tip toward the new system; a critical number of opinion leaders and groups commit themselves to the new system and take more risks to make changes in crucial places.

Emergence of new infrastructure: Some elements of the system are operated in keeping with the desired new system. These new ways are generally accepted.

Predominance of the new system: The more powerful elements of the system operate as defined by the new system. Key leaders begin envisioning even better systems.

Systemic change occurs when inequitable policies, procedures and attitudes are changed, promoting equity and access to educational opportunities for all students. Such change happens through the sustained involvement of all critical players in the school setting, including and often led by school counselors. Leadership, advocacy and collaboration are key strategies that are needed to create systemic change.

Examples of systemic change that promote equitable treatment of all students include changes in policies, procedures and attitudes that:
- Remove barriers to access to rigorous courses and learning paths for college and career readiness for all students
- Increase access to educational opportunities
- Create clear guidelines for addressing inappropriate behavior such as bullying and harassment
- Increase awareness of school safety issues
- Promote knowledge and skills for working in a diverse and multicultural work setting
- Address over- or underrepresentation of specific groups in programs such as special education, honors, Advanced Placement and International Baccalaureate
- Model inclusive language

- Create an environment that encourages any student or group to feel comfortable to come forward with problems (ASCA, 2006)

Success resulting from systemic change can be measured by the closing of achievement, opportunity and attainment gaps. Examples of success in changes for all student groups such as:
- Increased promotion and graduation rates
- Decreased discipline or suspension rates
- Increased attendance at school
- Increased attendance in educational opportunities
- Increased numbers of students completing high school college and career ready

School counseling programs can create change. School counseling programs that promote data-driven change designed to meet the needs of students can be the initiator of systemic change that has a positive impact on all students in the school – and the academic outcomes of all students in the school.

LEADERSHIP

By Anita Young, Ph.D., Assistant Professor, Johns Hopkins University

Now more than ever before, school counselors have the opportunity – and the responsibility – to assume leadership roles in their schools that positively affect student outcomes. Once thought to be the job of administrators, advancing academic achievement, reducing barriers to learning and creating equitable learning environments are central priorities for school counselors. As one of the four major ASCA National Model themes, leadership enhances school counselors' ability to implement and sustain data-driven comprehensive school counseling programs and is an essential element of all four components of the ASCA National Model.

School counselor leaders are culturally responsive change agents who integrate instructional and school counseling best practices to initiate, develop and implement equitable services and programs for all students. They are skilled at counseling, advocating, teaming and collaborating and using data to promote student success. School counselor leaders are also able to construct meaning from their personal and professional experiences to bring about substantive change for all students. Whether at the elementary, middle or high school level, all school counselors have the ability lead. While there are many leadership characteristics and practices, utilizing effective school counselor leadership requires:
- visionary thinking
- challenging inequities
- shared decision making
- collaborative processing
- modeling excellence
- a courageous stance

Leadership and foundation: The first order of business for school counselor leaders is to create a school counseling vision and mission aligned with the school's vision and mission, which grounds the development of a data-driven comprehensive school counseling program and underscores the impact of leadership. An effective school counselor leader drives discussions about high expectations for all students, assumes responsibility to facilitate professional development activities pertaining to beliefs about student learning and ensures the student standards are used as a measure to assess students' progress. Leading the vision also necessitates the ability to articulate the school counseling vision and mission and influence others to develop compelling program goals.

Leadership and management: The assessments and tools of the management component help school counselor leaders create equitable services for all students. Leadership within the management component is demonstrated by training colleagues to collect, organize and target data that will lead to meaningful data analysis of program outcomes desired in the accountability component. These data may lead to rethinking current processes to mobilize more efficient services needed for students and to advocate for system change.

School counselor leaders are effective managers of resources and programs. Leadership capacity is demonstrated within the management component by accepting ownership of school counseling programs, encouraging others to lead and sharing resources. School counselor leaders understand the big picture of organizational processes and value collaborative outcomes. Espousing leadership means giving voice to the benefits of school counseling interventions and ensuring the need for school counselor presence on leadership teams is clearly articulated. For example, a school counselor leader might assume responsibility for the development of the program calendar, create the annual agreement, organize and facilitate advisory council meetings, develop action plans or simply ensure there is representation on the school improvement plan, faculty advisory committee and parent-teacher-student association.

Leadership and delivery: Effective school counselors are skilled at delivering direct academic, career and personal/social services to students including curriculum, providing individual student planning and responsive services. Effective school counselor leaders ensure the core school counseling curriculum is data-driven and are champions in articulating outcomes to stakeholders.

School counselor leaders have a profound impact on systemic change through indirect services to students such as collaborating and consulting with stakeholders. The magnitude of school counselor engagement and commitment to lead is often exhibited through a willingness to collaborate with others. The process of identifying program goals, improving learning and meeting the needs of all students can occur through collaborative dialogue with parents and guardians, administrators, teachers and community members. School counselor leadership means forming relationships and acquiring mutual respect for stakeholder opinions to support all students' academic success. The presence of collaborative processes, partnerships and practices can also contribute to sustained learning outcomes that help students achieve at higher levels.

School counselor leaders use data to determine how to maximize the amount of time spent in direct and indirect student services to produce the greatest impact on student achievement and success, thus keeping program management tasks and unrelated responsibilities at minimum. Examples of school counselors building leadership capacity that promotes direct and indirect services are listed but not limited to the suggestions below:

- develop programs promoting college, career and citizenship readiness
- evaluate existing preventive counseling services
- use data as a guide to tell the story about student needs
- inspire and motivate others to lead data-driven responsive services
- launch a schoolwide crisis response plan
- multitask and create multiple opportunities to execute the mission
- initiate collaborative business and community partnerships

Leadership and accountability: The accountability component links curriculum, small-group and closing-the-gap results to systemic change for all students. School counselor leaders can use the results analyses to demonstrate the effectiveness of school counseling program interventions and to guide program improvement. Additionally, school counselor leaders can use the school counselor performance appraisal template to inform supervisors of an evaluative tool appropriate for school counselors. Critical to an accountable school counselor leader is the ability to chart the direction for continuous personal and professional improvement. Reflective statements a school counselor leader might contemplate are:

- Persuasive strategies that I use to gain buy-in are....
- I respond to social justice inequities by .....
- My vision for the school counseling program is ....
- I consider myself a leader because .....
- I consistently use and analyze data to....
- When I encounter barriers that might impede student success, I ....
- I am proficient in the use of data and share my expertise by ....

In summary, the acceptance and demonstration of effective leadership practices can contribute to a school counselor's self-efficacy and professional identity. School counselor leadership is visible at all levels, and its transformative power cannot be underestimated.

ADVOCACY AND SOCIAL JUSTICE

By Trish Hatch, Ph.D., Associate Professor of Counseling and School Psychology, San Diego State University

School counselors implementing the ASCA National Model work toward socially just outcomes by acting on the themes of the ASCA National Model as leaders, advocates, collaborators and systemic change agents. They ensure equity and access for all students to reach their full potential in K-12 schools and beyond. The ASCA Ethical Standards for School Counselors call on school counselors to advocate for, lead and create equity-based school counseling programs that help close achievement, opportunity and attainment gaps. These gaps deny students access and opportunities to pursue career and college goals. Ethical school counselors are advocates ensuring access to rigorous college- and career-readiness curriculum and have high expectations for every student. As motivated agents of change, they utilize data to prevent and remove environmental and institutional barriers that deny students high-level academic, career and college access and personal/social opportunities.

School counselors are advocates for socially just outcomes when they:
- Actively seek to expand their cultural competence and commitment to social justice advocacy, knowledge and skills
- Develop their cultural proficiency as educational leaders who acknowledge how prejudice, power and various forms of oppression affect students
- Disaggregate attendance, behavior, grades, course-taking patterns and other types of achievement data with a special focus on diverse populations
- Address inequitable policies, procedures or instructional conditions that may impede the academic achievement, college access, career readiness or personal/social development of students
- Contribute to creating systemic change and necessary educational reform that promotes equitable access to rigorous educational opportunities, family engagement and school and community relationships.

Through the foundation of the ASCA National Model, socially just school counseling programs include advocacy for equity and access for all students to achieve at high levels through their mission and vision statements. School counselors disaggregate academic and behavioral data to uncover any discrepancies and then set program goals to close achievement, opportunity and attainment gaps with data-driven interventions. Program goals include delivering the school counseling core curriculum to every student with particular attention to ensuring competency attainment for underrepresented, underserved and underperforming students.

Through the delivery system, socially just school counseling programs include a focus on equity, not equality. In addition to ensuring each student receives the school counseling core curriculum, special consideration is given to students who may benefit from additional curriculum, group or individual counseling to master student competencies. Other equity-focused curriculum delivery examples include scheduling additional college nights for first-generation college-going families, ensuring translation for bilingual students, providing information on LGBTQ-friendly campuses and featuring diverse alumni to answer career and college access questions. Individual student planning includes an annual guaranteed time to support the students' and parents' understanding of the full magnitude of their educational choices, future opportunities, access to rigorous academics and learning paths for career and college.

Through program management, socially just school counseling programs include action plans that help close achievement, opportunity and attainment gaps. School counselors use data to determine which students require academic or behavioral interventions and ensure interventions for high-needs students and underrepresented groups. They manage their time by limiting non-school-counseling activities; they ensure the annual agreement with their administrator includes calendared activities for interventions and regular professional development to improve their cultural proficiency. School counselors ensure there is culturally diverse representation on the advisory council and advocate for funding to support access to necessary resources such as technology for students who can't afford computers and multiple-language documents for bilingual students and families.

Through accountability, socially just school counseling programs demonstrate results in closing achievement, opportunity and attainment gaps through closing-the-gap results reports and program improvement decisions. School counselors self-evaluate their performance in light of how equitable their professional practices have been. They celebrate success for all, not for few. They advocate for the system to change in response to student needs, rather than assuming students will change or limit their goals and dreams. When analyzing data, school counselors may realize the "intervention" students need is not a small group or individual counseling but rather the school counselor's advocacy to change an existing educational policy, procedure or practice that may be contributing to student inequities and denying students access to opportunities. These system change issues include addressing the following concerns:
- Disproportionate discipline rates for boys, students of color, students with disabilities
- Low percentages of poor/working class students taking college placement exams
- Students assigned lunch and recess detention for lack of homework completion
- Disproportionate numbers of students of color or males suspended or expelled
- High numbers of bilingual students scoring low on state exams

- Boys of color overrepresented in special education
- Underrepresentation of students of color in advanced courses
- Race/ethnicity, social class, ability/disability and gender gaps in students graduating college-eligible
- Lack of multiple measures or school counselor voice in student course placement decisions
- Limited Advanced Placement, International Baccalaureate and honors course availability and course prerequisite barriers
- Lack of bilingual college and career preparation materials
- Retention policies that offer little remediation or support opportunities
- Summer school availability only for those who can fund it themselves
- Attendance policies that assign an "F" to students with 10 or more absences (without remedial opportunities)

Socially just interventions for system change can have a greater impact on students than individual or group counseling alone. By using data to tell their story, school counselors can speak to the current condition, provide students examples and advocate for programs, policies and practices promoting achievement and success for all students.

To effectively partner in student achievement, school counselors must possess the knowledge, attitudes and skills to demonstrate leadership in diverse schools. School counselors must use culturally proficient skills to challenge the status quo and existing belief systems and discuss challenging issues of equity and access with school stakeholders. This may require recruiting like-minded professionals to create data teams that commit to reviewing disaggregated data and school policies regularly. School counselors as advocates use their voice to address institutional oppressions and systems that have historically disenfranchised certain students. Every interaction is an equity-focused change agent opportunity.

COLLABORATION

By Patti Kinney, Associate Director, Middle Level Services, National Association of Secondary School Principals

Probably few jobs in education have evolved as much in terms of duties and responsibilities as that of the school counselor. In the past, school counselors, especially in upper grade levels, have often been relegated to "administrivia" duties, responsible for record keeping, report writing, test administration, scheduling and other "duties as assigned." In today's world, it's critical that schools look beyond these tasks, take advantage of a school counselor's expertise and work collaboratively to build a school culture that promotes the success of each student served by the school.

Although the school principal may serve as the head of the school and ultimately be responsible for student success, the school counselor plays a critical role in making student success a reality. Principals need school counselors' perspective and leadership in working together on behalf of the students in the school. Teachers need school counselors' skills and specific knowledge to work effectively with students, especially ones with special needs such as learning disabilities, family issues, emotional and social difficulties and/or health problems. School counselors must be the ever-present voice to ensure student needs are recognized and the staff knows how to access additional help or resources when needed.

Additionally, the entire school community must work together to create schools that are physically and emotionally safe for all. Teachers must feel safe to express opinions, take initiative in solving problems and continually try to find more effective ways to help students be successful. Parents must feel welcomed at the school and that their voice is valued. Anonymity must be banished, and students must feel safe to question, explore and achieve. Who better to help with this than the school counselor?

School counselors should ask themselves:
- Are you collaborating with teachers to help improve student behavior?
- Are you leading the way to find, create and implement anti-bullying and harassment programs?

- Have you helped establish a conflict resolution curriculum? An advisory program?
- Do you provide support to staff on working effectively with students with special needs?
- Do you run small groups to help students cope with specific issues?

The list goes on and on. School counselors must take responsibility to let the school know what they are capable of doing and work together to set these types of programs in place. The success of students depends on it.

There should be no stronger student advocate than school counselors. They must be the heart and soul of the school and lead the charge in creating a school culture that promotes an equitable education for every student. Being able to access the data and look at it from a larger viewpoint puts school counselors in an excellent position to help the school determine if its programs, practices and policies ensure social and programmatic equity for all. School counselors can begin this examination by asking:
- To what extent is the enrollment in courses or programs for gifted and talented, special education, English language learners, etc. reflective of the school's demographics?
- Does the percentage of students achieving at a proficient or higher level of performance reflect the demographics of the entire school?
- Does the school's recognition system value diversity, service and academic achievement?
- Does the percentage of students receiving recognition reflect the demographics of the student body?
- Do the school's discipline statistics reflect the demographics of the student body, or are some subgroups over- or underrepresented?

Although the role of the school counselor may have changed over the years, one thing has remained steady – the vast majority of school counselors are in their role because they care for children. In today's world, school counselors are in the perfect position to both support and lead the collaboration needed to achieve student success and to ensure student needs remain in the center of all decisions. They should serve as the school's conscience by continually asking:
- Is this good for kids?
- Will this help our students succeed?
- Are we doing this for students or for ourselves?

Sitting Bull, a wise Native American chief, understood the power of collaborating on behalf of youth when he said, "We must put our minds together and see what life we can make for our children." Principals can't do it alone, school counselors can't, staff can't, parents can't, community services can't. It's only by working together that a school community will make a better life for the students it serves.

SYSTEMIC CHANGE

By Glenn Cook, Publisher, American School Board Journal, National School Boards Association

We know the ingredients of successful schools: A strong instructional leader; a caring, committed, and knowledgeable staff; an engaged community; and high expectations for all students. Thanks to a growing body of research, we also are learning more about what makes an effective school board and how that results in high-achieving districts.

Not surprisingly, the use of data is important on both counts to create systemic change.

School counselors who are focused on systemic change know how individual students are performing. They know, through data analysis and collaborative work with other facets of the school leadership team, what is necessary to improve the achievement of individual students.

For school boards, data serve as a leadership tool that helps its members answer larger, broader questions. Board members don't need to know specific test scores or instructional needs of individual students. However, they must know the right questions to ask to ensure all students have equal access to a rigorous curriculum and the support necessary to succeed.

Data-savvy school boards also know this fact: Comprehensive school counseling programs that advocate for every student can prevent dropouts and maximize access to education options beyond high school. A 2011 Center for Public Education report notes that dropout prevention programs work when school counselors "build sustained relationships with students, closely monitor each student's attendance and performance, intervene rapidly at the first sign of trouble, help students and families overcome obstacles to educational success and teach students how to solve problems."

Like the ASCA National Model, the National School Boards Association's Key Work of School Boards provides a framework for local boards to effect systemic change, improve student achievement and engage their communities. Eight interrelated action areas help focus the board's work at the local level:

- **Vision:** Statements identifying the school district's future, intermediate and short-term goals, associated objectives and supporting tasks. Developing a shared vision for student achievement is the starting point for a school board and its community.
- **Standards:** Statements that define and explain educational expectations for all grade levels and that support the district's vision statements. Standards form the foundation for a school district's learning system.
- **Assessment:** Identified tools and processes that measure educational outcomes against stated standards. A sound local assessment system incorporates multiple assessments, alignment with academic standards, coordination with state assessment programs and both "lagging" and "leading" indicators.
- **Accountability:** Assigned responsibility for educational outcomes. A strong accountability process focuses on improved student achievement as measured by comprehensive data collection and analysis.
- **Alignment:** Resource allocation, communication, planning and program implementation all work together to support the district's vision, goals and priorities.
- **Climate:** The educational environment that creates the conditions for successful teaching and learning.
- **Collaboration and community engagement:** Established trust and confidence among all educational stakeholders. Necessary partners for school districts include parents, business and political leaders, media representatives and other citizens in the community.
- **Continuous improvement:** Constantly seeking and planning new ways to improve the system. Good data empower the board and staff to refine, strengthen, modify, correct and/or eliminate existing programs and practices to get better results.

For more information, visit *www.nsba.org/Board-Leadership/Governance/KeyWork.aspx*

It is tempting, in a data-driven world, to ignore the outside forces – emotional, social, physical and economic – that can become barriers to increased student achievement. That is one reason school counseling is so important. Working together collaboratively, using data mixed with common sense, is necessary to create systemic change and improve achievement for all.

Foundation

Topics Include:

Program Focus
- Beliefs
- Vision Statement
- Mission Statement
- Program Goals

Student Competencies
- ASCA Student Standards
- Other Student Standards

Professional Competencies
- School Counselor Professional Competencies
- ASCA Ethical Standards for School Counselors

Introduction

The school counseling program's foundation serves as the solid ground upon which the rest of the comprehensive school counseling program is built. The decisions made as the foundation is being developed or modified become the "what" of the program. The "what" is defined as the student knowledge, attitudes and skills that are learned because of a school counseling program. Designing a strong foundation requires a collaborative effort with staff, parents/guardians and the community to determine what every student will receive as a benefit of a school counseling program.

The purpose of this component of the ASCA National Model is to establish the focus of the comprehensive school counseling program based on the academic, career and personal/social needs of the students in the school. Elements of the foundation include three sections:
- Program Focus
- Student Competencies
- Professional Competencies

PROGRAM FOCUS

Beliefs

Everyone has beliefs. Beliefs are personal and individual and are derived from our backgrounds and experiences. But most importantly, our beliefs drive our behavior.

Beliefs are discussed early in the process of developing a school counseling program. It is clear that school counselors' beliefs about students, families, teachers and the educational process are crucial in supporting student success. Open, honest dialogue is required to ensure school counseling teams and departments explore complex issues from many points of view.

When working with a school counseling team, it is important for each team member to contribute to the discussion on beliefs to come to a common understanding about each other's point of view.

Effective school counseling belief statements:
- Indicate agreed-upon beliefs about the ability of all students to achieve
- Address how the school counseling program meets student developmental needs
- Address the school counselor's role as an advocate for every student
- Identify persons to be involved in the planning, managing, delivery and evaluation of school counseling program activities
- Include how data inform program decisions
- Include how ethical standards guide the work of school counselors

Exercise: Developing Beliefs
Each team member should contribute to the beliefs discussion. The following questions will help your team complete the chart:
1. What do we believe about the ability of all students to achieve?
2. How do we address developmental needs of all students?
3. What is the school counselor's role as an advocate for every student?
4. Who do we believe is involved in the planning, managing, delivery and evaluation of program activities?
5. How are data used to inform program decisions?
6. How do ethical standards guide the work of school counselors?

Following the discussion, define and record the group's beliefs.

Belief	This belief is important for students because...	What this belief means for the program	What this belief means the school counselor will do

Sample Beliefs

School counselors in the Everett Naismith Middle School Counseling Program believe:

- All students can achieve and meet high standards that will result in college and career success
- Student developmental needs are best met by implementing a comprehensive school counseling program
- School counselors must be leaders, advocates and collaborators who create equitable access to rigorous curriculum and opportunities for self-directed personal growth for every student
- Student achievement is maximized by participation in a comprehensive school counseling program that is planned, managed, delivered and evaluated by licensed professional school counselors
- Data must be analyzed and translated into goals that guide the development of the comprehensive school counseling program promoting student achievement
- Applying the ASCA Ethical Standards for School Counselors empowers school counselors to make decisions based on the highest moral principles to promote the maximum development of every student

Vision Statement

Vision focuses on the future, more specifically, a preferred or desired future (Levin, 2000). When discussing the vision of a school counseling program, school counselors communicate what they want to see in the future for the school community related to student achievement and other student outcomes. A discussion about vision builds off of the discussion of beliefs and becomes the picture of what school counselors hope to see in the next five to 10 years (National School Boards Association [NSBA], 2009).

School counselors can promote the success of every student by developing a vision of learning for all students that is shared and supported by stakeholders (The Council of Chief State School Officers, 2008). This vision "ensures that equitable academic, career, post-secondary access and personal/social opportunities for all students through the use of data to help close achievement gaps and opportunity gaps" is clearly articulated in a vision statement (ASCA, 2010).

The vision statement for the school counseling program aligns with the vision of the school and district. It describes not what we are but what we want to become and what life will be like for students, staff, parents and stakeholders from the perspective of the school counselor (NSBA, 2009). It is shaped by how school counselors view the world and reflects what they believe about students, families, teachers and the educational process that drive their ability to support success for all students (Dahir & Stone, 2012).

A review of research shows that a shared vision or mission is "a characteristic of effective schools, helps foster inclusive and equitable schools, directs positive school change and ideally guides quality professional development" (Kose, 2011, p. 120). All of these areas fit within a comprehensive school counseling program. A clearly formed vision statement shapes school counselors' actions, instills their work with meaning and reminds them why they are in the profession (Leithwood & Hallinger, 2002).

An effective vision statement:

- Describes a future world where the school counseling goals and strategies are being successfully achieved
- Outlines a rich and textual picture of what success looks like and feels like
- Is bold and inspiring
- States the best possible student outcomes that are five to 15 years away
- Is believable and achievable (Kose, 2011; Levin, 2000)

Sample Vision Statement
The students at Everett Naismith Middle School are high-achieving learners who graduate college and career ready, well prepared to meet the challenges and high expectations of the 21st century. All students participate in rigorous curriculum and high-quality opportunities for self-directed personal growth supported by the comprehensive school counseling program that facilitates strategic partnerships between the school, family and community. As successful, life-long learners and productive citizens, our students achieve their fullest potential, making a positive difference in our school and community.

Mission Statement

A mission statement provides the focus and direction to reach the vision, creating one focus or purpose in the development and implementation of the comprehensive school counseling program. The school counseling mission statement aligns with and is a subset of the school and district's mission. Therefore, the school counseling program supports the learning environment and at the same time makes unique contributions to meeting students' needs and nurturing their growth.

The program's mission statement is clear, concise and specific to the program's intent and what the program will contribute to the overall mission of schools.

An effective mission statement:

- Aligns with the school's mission statement and may show linkages to district and state department of education mission statements
- Is written with students as the primary focus
- Advocates for equity, access and success of every student
- Indicates the long-range results desired for all students

Sample School Mission Statement
The mission of Clinton High School, as a diverse and caring community, is to use a challenging and relevant curriculum to help all students to be successful, lifelong learners and problem solvers.

Adapted from Clinton High School (Iowa), 2012

Sample School Counseling Mission Statement
The mission of the school counseling program is to provide all students with a comprehensive school counseling program centered around an engaging curriculum that encourages the highest level of student achievement through their growth in academic, career and personal/social domains. In partnership with teachers, administrators, parents and a caring

community, the school counselors will help all students to be successful lifelong learners and problem solvers.

Adapted from Clinton High School (Iowa), 2012

Program Goals

Program goals define how the vision and mission will be accomplished and guide the development of curriculum, small-group and closing-the-gap action plans. School counseling program goals are statements about a desirable outcome toward which the program is willing to devote resources (Dimmit, Carey, & Hatch, 2007). These goal statements address specific student outcomes, including improved student achievement, attendance, behavior and school safety through one or more of the three domains: academic, career or personal/social development.

Program goals are based on school data and, in many cases, focus attention on issues related to an achievement, opportunity or attainment gap. Goal setting, based on school-specific data and aligned with the school counseling vision and mission, gives focus to the school counseling program. Typically program goals are developed at the beginning of the school year.

Effective program goals
- Promote achievement, attendance, behavior and/or school safety
- Are based on school data
- Address schoolwide data, policies and practices or address closing-the-gap issues
- Address academic, career and/or personal/social development

The SMART goal format (Doran, 1981) is frequently used for writing program goals. SMART is an acronym for specific, measurable, attainable, results-oriented and time bound. This acronym is often used to help an individual identify goals and the necessary steps needed to accomplish a given tasks.

Goal Setting: The Process

The goal-setting process often begins by identifying a "burning question" related to educational issues (Young & Kaffenberger, 2009). It builds on courageous conversations about beliefs about student learning and student inequalities and is founded in data such as student enrollment patterns in rigorous classes, incidences of discipline referrals or student absences (Dimmitt, Carey, & Hatch, 2007; Haycock, 2001; Marzano, 2010; Singleton & Linton, 2006).

Although there may be many ways to identify a goal, the following process suggests four ways to examine data elements.

1. Examine the school data profile to identify academic gaps by categories such as race/ethnicity, gender, age or grade level.

2. List current academic, career and personal/social domain activities and interventions provided to all students. (See Brainstorming Activity p 27.) The brainstorming activity can help school counselors provide a cursory review of their comprehensive services and consider gaps in their program delivery (Bauman, 2004; Singleton & Linton, 2006; Young & Kaffenberger, 2009).

3. Identify a specific school improvement plan goal and consider the school counseling program activities that align with the school's instructional accountability goals. Have a discussion with the principal about his/her goals. Principals are often working toward specific goals from the school improvement plan, and it may be timesaving for school counselors to understand the principal's focus for the year.

4. Complete the school counseling program SMART goals worksheet. (See School Counseling Program SMART Goals p. 28).

Sample Goal-Setting Process for Academic Goals
1. School Data Profile Review
   Benton High School has traditionally been highly competitive in academic grades, high school exit exam scores, end-of-course exam scores and performance on college entrance exams such as SAT and ACT. In the past few years, the average SAT and ACT scores have declined well below the national average and showed an achievement gap for African-American students especially in mathematics.
2. Current Strategies
   a. Students and parents are provided with resources on college entrance exams.
   b. Data are analyzed to determine which students may need additional support to prepare for college entrance exams.
   c. School counselors collaborate with the teachers and administrators to identify additional support for mathematics for students who need assistance.
3. School Improvement Plan
   The school improvement plan includes a goal to improve SAT/ACT scores for all students.
4. SMART Goal Development
   The following SMART goals are potential goals addressing school data.
   ▪ By the end of year, the school's average SAT and ACT score will increase by 10 percent.
   ▪ By the end of year two, the achievement gap in mathematics for African-American students will decrease by 50 percent.
   ▪ By the end of year three, the school's average score on SAT and ACT exams will exceed the national average for all subgroups in the school.

Sample Goal Setting Process for Attendance Goals
1. School Data Profile Review
   The district provides the school with daily attendance reports identifying which students have been absent. At the end of the school year, the school receives a report identifying students with eight or more absences for the year. The school counselors review the reports and identify 73 students with eight or more absences.

2. Current Strategies
   a. Letters are sent to the homes of students with four, seven and 10 absences.
   b. Students are considered for retention if they have 20 or more absences.
3. School Improvement Plan
   A goal of increased attendance is a part of the plan.
4. SMART Goal Development
   The following goal was developed.
   Students with 10 or more absences in the previous year will have fewer than eight absences this year.

These sample goals promote the academic domain by focusing on an increase in academic achievement, success on college entrance exams and increased attendance. The goals are simple, yet precise. (Young & Kaffenberger, 2009)

Brainstorming Activity

Academic	Career	Personal/Social

Sample School Counseling Program
SMART Goals Worksheet

Specific Issue What is the specific issue based on our school's data?	
Measurable How will we measure the effectiveness of our interventions?	
Attainable What outcome would stretch us but is still attainable?	
Results-Oriented Is the goal reported in results-oriented data (process, perception and outcome)?	
Time Bound When will our goal be accomplished?	

School:_____ Year: _____

School Counselor(s): _____

Based on the information above, write a single goal statement sentence
Example: By the end of the year, the number of discipline referrals will decrease by 20 percent.

_____

_____

_____

_____

STUDENT COMPETENCIES

ASCA Student Standards

ASCA Student Standards (available at *www.ASCANationalModel.org*) identify and prioritize the specific knowledge, attitudes and skills that students should be able to demonstrate as a result of a school counseling program. School counselors use the standards to assess student growth and development, guide the development of strategies and activities and create a program that helps students achieve their highest potential.

The ASCA Student Standards are organized in three broad domains to promote behaviors that enhance the learning process: academic, career and personal/social development. Standards for each domain provide guidance and direction for states, school systems and individual schools for the development of effective school counseling programs. Student competencies define the specific knowledge, attitudes and skills students should obtain, and indicators demonstrate skill acquisitions.

School-specific competencies and indicators from the ASCA Student Standards are the foundation for classroom lessons, small groups and activities with a school counseling program. The competencies and indicators directly reflect the school counseling program, mission and goals. The ASCA Student Standards are aligned with district, state and/or national documents to reflect the district's local priorities.

Use the ASCA Student Standards program planning tool (available at *www.ASCA NationalModel.org*) to identify grade-level specific competencies and indicators for the school counseling program.

Other Student Standards

District and state initiatives often contain educational standards for students other than the ASCA Student Standards. School counselors are encouraged to consider how these other student standards complement and inform their school counseling program and, if appropriate, select competencies from these other standards that align with ASCA Student Standards and their school counseling program's mission and goals.

The following are examples of other student standards.
- Framework for 21st Century Learning, *www.p21.org/*
- The National Career Development Guidelines, *www.ncda.org*
- The Six Pillars of Character, *www.charactercounts.org/*
- State standards (check state department of education Web sites)

PROFESSIONAL COMPETENCIES

ASCA School Counselor Competencies

The ASCA School Counselor Competencies outline the knowledge, attitudes and skills that ensure school counselors are equipped to meet the rigorous demands of the profession and the needs of our preK-12 students. These competencies are necessary to ensure the future school counselor workforce is able to continue to make a positive difference in students' lives.

The competencies are applicable along a continuum of areas. For instance, school counselor education programs may use the competencies as benchmarks for ensuring students graduate with the knowledge, attitudes and skills needed for developing and implementing school counseling programs. School counselors use the ASCA School Counselor Competencies as a checklist to self-evaluate their own competencies and, as a result, formulate an appropriate professional development plan. (See ASCA School Counselor Competencies, p. 148.)

ASCA Ethical Standards for School Counselors

Ethics are the customs, norms, standards and accepted practice of the school counseling profession (Corey, Corey, & Callanan, 2010). The ASCA Ethical Standards for School Counselors (2010) specify the principles of ethical behavior necessary to maintain the highest standard of integrity, leadership and professionalism. They guide school counselors' decision-making and help standardize professional practice to protect both students and school counselors.

Ethical decision-making models provide direction to school counselors when faced with an ethical dilemma. The use of a professionally structured decision-making process ensures a consistent and fair standard of practice is used in addressing an ethical dilemma. ASCA's Ethical Standards include a nine-step process for ethical decision making.

1. Define the problem emotionally and intellectually
2. Apply the ASCA Ethical Standards and the law
3. Consider the students' chronological and developmental levels
4. Consider the setting, parental rights and minors' rights
5. Apply the moral principles
6. Determine your potential courses of action and their consequences
7. Evaluate the selected action
8. Consult
9. Implement the course of action

To read ASCA's Ethical Standards for School Counselors, go to *www.schoolcounselor.org/ethics*.

References

American School Counseling Association. (2010). *Ethical standards for school counselors.* Alexandria, VA: Author.

Bauman, S. (2004). School counselors and research revisited. *Professional School Counseling, 7,* 141-151.

Corey, G., Corey, M. S., & Callanan, P. (2010). *Issues and ethics in the helping profession.* Pacific Grove, CA: Brooks/Cole.

Dahir, C. A. & Stone, C. B. (2012). *The transformed school counselor* (2nd ed.). Belmont, CA: Brooks/Cole.

Dimmitt, C., Carey, J. C. & Hatch, T. (2007). Evidence-based school counseling: Making a difference with data-driven practices. Thousand Oaks, CA: Corwin Press.

Dollarhide, C. T. & Saginak, K. A. (2012). *Comprehensive school counseling programs: K-12 delivery systems in action* (2nd ed.). Upper Saddle River, NJ: Pearson Education, Inc.

Doran, G. T. (1981). There's a S.M.A.R.T. way to write management's goals and objectives. *Management Review, 70*(11), 35-36.

Haycock, K. (2001). Closing the achievement gap. *Educational Leadership, 58,* 6-11.

Kose, B. W. (2011). Developing a transformative school vision: Lessons from peer-nominated principals. *Education and Urban Society, 43*(2), 119-136.

Leithwood, K., & Hallinger, P. (Senior Co-eds.; 2002). *The second international handbook of educational leadership and administration.* Dordrecht, Netherlands: Kluwer Press.

Levin, I. M. (2000). *Vision revisited: Telling the story of the future.* The Journal of Applied Behavioral Science, 36(1), 91-107.

Marzano, R. (2010). High expectations for all. *Educational Leadership, 68,* 82-85.

National School Boards Association (2009). *The key works of school boards guidebook.* Alexandria, VA: Author.

Singleton, G. E., & Linton, C. (2006). *Courageous conversations about race.* Thousand Oaks, CA: Corwin Press.

The Council of Chief State School Officers. (2008). *Educational leadership policy standards: ISLLC 2008.* Washington, DC; Author.

Young, A. & Kaffenberger, C. (2009) *Making data work* (2nd ed.). Alexandria, VA: American School Counselor Association.

BELIEFS MATTER

By Mark Kuranz, Director of Professional Development, ASCA, and Rachelle Perusse, Ph.D., Associate Professor, University of Connecticut

The school counselor's beliefs are the engine powering the school counseling program. If school counselors do not believe in high expectations, rigorous course planning, post-secondary/career planning, and a safe and respectful learning environment for all students, they will not advocate for a school counseling program that serves all students. In essence, their lack of belief in all students maintains the status quo.

Beliefs drive behaviors, and school counselors must continuously ask themselves how they view all students in the school. If school counselors do not believe in supporting all students, they will not behave in ways that are helpful for all students. Our beliefs drive advocacy.

Beliefs are addressed in the foundation section of the ASCA National Model when considering your program's philosophy and mission statement. Historically, some students have been left out of the recipe for a successful school experience because school staff did not believe all students could learn. Today in the Foundation of the ASCA National Model, belief statements address the discrepancies in the school data profile. These beliefs must not be kept a secret but shared with school counseling peers, where a clear statement can be articulated to other school personnel and the greater community.

Collaboration is critical to defining beliefs. School counselors must commit to continually engaging in these discussions and commit to self-reflection to ensure their beliefs are consistent with the mission of the school.

Systemic change requires school counselors to be aware of their beliefs, share their beliefs with others and ensure the shared beliefs drive change in school practices, procedures and policies that disenfranchise students.

Self-check:

- What do you believe about student achievement for all students?
- Do you believe all students can achieve to high standards?
- Are you expecting all students to achieve to high standards?
- What behaviors do you exhibit that communicate high expectations matter?
- What school practices demonstrate the belief that all students can achieve to high standards?
- Are you providing the resources for all students to be successful?
- What resources are available and necessary to support student success?
- How can your time be prioritized and managed to improve school success?
- What are the outcomes for you in understanding that beliefs matter?

SCHOOL COUNSELORS' ROLE IN WORKING WITH LGBTQ STUDENTS

By Vincent Pompei, School Counselor, Val Verde Unified, San Diego, Calif., and LGBTQ Consultant

Students who are or are perceived to be lesbian, gay, bisexual, transgender or questioning (LGBTQ) are often targets of bullying, harassment and violence. These students frequently lack feelings of connectedness and safety at school, and their experiences have been linked to absenteeism, drop out, mental health issues, drug and alcohol abuse, lower future aspirations and suicide risks. School counselors play a vital role in creating a safe, inclusive and welcoming school climate for LGBTQ students and students of same-sex parents.

The ASCA National Model is a framework for school counseling programs designed to meet the needs of all students, including those who identify as or are perceived to be LGBTQ. Implementing the ASCA National Model can ensure LGBTQ students' unique needs are met.

Foundation: When writing belief statements about the ability of all students to succeed, consider LGBTQ students' unique needs and challenges. When writing your vision and mission statements, include LGBTQ students if specific groups are listed. If "all students" is used in the vision statement, give consideration to how school counselors ensure LGBTQ students have an equitable chance at achieving the vision. Effective vision and mission statements advocate for equity, access and success of every student.

Building on the mission and vision, program goals can be created that include desirable outcomes for LGBTQ students. Examples include:
- Increase school connectedness, feelings of safety, personal well-being, academic achievement, attendance rate, college/career readiness and graduation rate for LGBTQ students.
- Decrease incidents of bullying, harassment and homophobia on school campus.

When selecting standards and competencies from the ASCA Student Standards to focus on, consider how they apply to LGBTQ students. Strategies may need to be tailored and additional emphasis may be needed on personal/social standards to ensure these students achieve their highest potential.

Professional competencies help ensure school counselors make a positive difference in the lives of all students. The ASCA Ethical Standards for School Counselors recommend school counselors receive training that helps them better advocate for, affirm and create an equitable and safe school climate for LGBTQ students. Developing these skills helps school counselors provide, and encourage other staff to create, visible safe spaces so LGBTQ students have several trusting adults to turn to for support.

Management: When inviting new members to the advisory council, consider an LGBTQ expert from the community who can bring helpful guidance and resources to the school. In addition, the school counseling program annual calendar may include activities and services important to LGBTQ students such as National Coming Out Day, The Day of Silence or LGBT History Month to help LGBTQ students feel connected and included.

Using data is essential to ensuring all students benefit from the school counseling program. School counselors ensure LGBTQ students feel safe in reporting harassment or incidents of homophobia and follow up to ensure the response to complaints was effective.

Monitoring academic performance and attendance rates may offer clues that an LGBTQ student is dealing with issues of fear. Monitoring the behavior files of students who are bullying or showing signs of homophobia may provide useful data on the school counseling program's effectiveness at curbing such behavior. In addition, analyzing school climate surveys can help to determine if prevention/interventions have been effective.

Delivery: Issues relevant to LGBTQ students are appropriate for many curriculum lessons delivered by school counselors as a part of the school counseling core curriculum. Classroom lessons pertaining to diversity, respect and bullying prevention, particularly if they contain the words "lesbian, gay, bisexual and transgender," help LGBTQ students feel included. Non-heteronormative and inclusive language helps to engage and connect lessons to all student groups. If there is a need, school counselors can follow up individually or in small groups to address any additional needs of LGBTQ students.

Individual student planning with LGBTQ students may include sharing information on LGBTQ-friendly colleges, listings of scholarships for LGBTQ students, Fortune 500 companies that value LGBTQ employees and other LGBTQ-focused resources.

Responsive services may provide support for self-acceptance, the coming-out process, dealing with peer or family rejection and resilience. Responsive services may also be needed for a student who is intolerant or showing signs of homophobia. As with any student, discipline consequences must remain separate from a school counselor's intervention plan.

School counselors provide indirect student services to promote student achievement and systemic change. School counselors advocate for enumerated anti-bullying policies that include sexual orientation and gender identity/expression, as these policies have been shown to decrease anti-LGBTQ harassment and bullying. School counselors also make referrals to students and parents for additional assistance or information. A referral may direct LGBTQ students and straight allies to organizations that guide in the formation of a gay and straight alliance or, if parents are unsupportive of their LGBTQ child, a referral to community groups such as Parents, Family and Friends of Lesbians and Gays may provide needed resources.

If longer-term counseling services are needed, it is important to refer the student and parent to an open and affirming therapist. Although some organizations practice reparative or conversion therapy when working with LGBTQ youth, ASCA and many other national medical and educational associations consider this harmful and inappropriate.

Accountability: Analyzing program result reports contributes to a more focused and effective program, serving as a measure to determine if the experience of LGBTQ students has improved. A review of the curriculum, small-group and closing-the-gap results reports related to issues important to LGBTQ students will help determine if program goals are being met.

Implementing the ASCA National Model while considering LGBTQ students' unique needs will create a safer, more welcoming and inclusive school climate.

MULTICULTURALISM AND THE ASCA NATIONAL MODEL

By Tim Grothaus, Ph.D., Associate Professor and School Counseling Coordinator, Old Dominion University

School counselors have tremendous challenges and also terrific opportunities presented to us by the increasing diversity in our schools and communities. Each of us has a constellation of cultural identities, such as our race, ethnicity, socioeconomic status, gender, sexual orientation, ability/disability, native language and country and spirituality. These cultural facets can have powerful effects on our attitudes, perspectives and behavior. Recognizing this, the ASCA Ethical Standards for School Counselors, the professional literature and numerous ASCA position statements call us to value, respect and be responsive to these cultural influences. As ethical and effective professionals, we can answer this charge by implementing culturally responsive ASCA National Model programs.

Our school counseling program will likely reflect our own commitment to growing in cultural competence. This exciting lifelong journey of improving our cultural awareness, knowledge and skills can start with examining our own cultural identities, biases and privileges. We may experience some discomfort realizing that our own behaviors are culturally influenced and not the only correct way to view or do things. Yet respecting and valuing others' cultures and not expecting them to "see and be like me" can send a potent and positive message to our students and stakeholders.

The best way to enhance cultural competence appears to be through immersing ourselves in diverse communities of friends and colleagues. We can also grow through active involvement in our school's neighboring community while networking with available cultural resources. Accessing cultural informants, such as stakeholders who are fluent in the cultures represented in our schools, can be helpful. In addition, participating in culturally sensitive supervision can contribute to our progress. All of these activities take time and effort but will likely yield great benefits.

Culturally responsive implementation of the ASCA National Model also addresses the problems and possibilities posed by the abundant array of cultural influences in our schools. This includes school counselors acting as advocates, leaders and collaborators working for systemic changes that promote equity and success for all students.

Specifically, in the foundation section, we can conceptualize the standards and competencies in a culturally sensitive fashion. The school counseling program's beliefs and vision statements can display the importance of all students being valued for who they are and our dedication to fostering a sense of belonging in our school community. This sense of mattering has been shown to be related to improved academic and behavioral success. In addition, our school counseling program's mission statement can clearly state our commitment to honor our students' cultures and to access the rich cultural resources in our communities.

The Management section of the school counseling program could include an annual agreement containing goals targeting the elimination of access and achievement inequities among cultural groups. It could also explain how we will make the school counseling program accessible to stakeholders by being available at times and places that parents/caretakers are able to see us and having our office and materials accessible for persons with disabilities. It is also important to communicate (through a translator if necessary) with stakeholders in their preferred language. We can create a multicultural school counseling program advisory committee, with representative membership from the school and community, to advise us on all aspects of the school experience. Our calendars should be accessible and reflect our inclusive and inviting services and programs, including highlighting our use of time. When we examine disaggregated school data, we will likely find inequities (e.g., some groups of students receiving more behavioral referrals, disproportionate representation in gifted programs and those receiving special education services, disparate graduation rates for different student groups). We can use the data to create action plans to challenge school policies and practices contributing to maintaining the inequitable status-quo. Without a dedication to advocacy, we are probably unwittingly part of the problem.

The Delivery section can showcase our efforts to systematically improve multicultural relations, not just between racial or ethnic groups but also with regard to social class, ability/disability, sexual orientation and other cultural identities. These efforts go hand-in-hand with our efforts to create a vibrant school climate where cultural richness and strengths are celebrated. We can also promote inclusive language and cultural recognition (e.g., using humankind vs. mankind, celebrating cultural holidays and having school décor that represents our student populations). The school counseling curriculum can feature culturally inclusive lessons relevant to students' lives delivered using culturally sensitive teaching and classroom-management methods. In addition, individual student planning is a key activity to counteract the ill effects of cultural bias in testing and the trend of students as young as six or seven years old eliminating career options based on race, ethnicity, gender, social class, etc. The responsive services we provide can include broaching the topic of culture when counseling in individual or group settings. This approach shows that discussing cultural aspects of the situation are welcome, rather than being silent about culture, which may indicate a lack of awareness or willingness to examine these important aspects of our experiences.

Indirect student services such as consultation and collaboration could include discussions about "code switching," which involves making situationally intelligent decisions about language and behavior in changing circumstances. Valuing code switching can indicate respect for the cultural richness of students' home lives, as can the use of culturally sensitive terms (e.g., requesting that students use "school" or "formal" English rather than "proper" English, which seems to imply a student's home language is improper). In addition, we can actively promote school-family-community collaboration, especially with parents/guardians who have been less involved, as this has been proven to benefit students.

The Accountability section can give us feedback about the cultural responsiveness of our services and whether our program is equitably serving all students. Our results reports can focus on the impact of the school counseling program over time in enhancing the cultural inclusiveness of the school climate and closing the pernicious gaps in achievement.

In sum, we are invited to be a learner among learners as we share the struggles and embrace and celebrate the cultural strengths of our school and community. Culturally competent implementation of the ASCA National Model will not only assist us in answering the question, "How are students different as a result of the school counseling program?" It will also enlighten us about how well we respect and respond to the rich cultural diversity present in our students and school community.

Management

To effectively deliver the school counseling curriculum and address the developmental needs of every student, the school counseling program must be effectively and efficiently managed. The management component of the ASCA National Model provides organizational assessments and tools designed to manage a school counseling program. The assessments and tools help school counselors develop, implement and evaluate their school counseling program based on clearly defined priorities reflecting student needs.

Topics Include:

Assessments
- School Counselor Competencies Assessment
- School Counseling Program Assessment
- Use-of-Time Assessment

Tools
- Annual Agreement
- Advisory Council
- Use of Data
- School Data Profile
- Program Results Data (Process, Perception and Outcomes)
- Curriculum, Small-Group and Closing-the-Gap Action Plans
- Lesson Plan
- Calendars

SCHOOL COUNSELOR COMPETENCIES ASSESSMENT

The school counselor competencies assessment supports school counselors' efforts to help students focus on academic, career and personal/social development so they achieve success in school and are prepared to lead fulfilling lives as responsible members of society. The assessment helps school counselors self-assess their knowledge, attitudes and skills necessary to perform the range of school counselor responsibilities in all four components of a comprehensive school counseling program.

The competencies are applicable in a variety of areas, including those listed on the following page.

School counselors	■ Self-assess their own competencies ■ Formulate an appropriate professional development plan
School administrators	■ Guide the recruitment and selection of competent school counselors ■ Develop or inform meaningful school counselor performance evaluation
School counselor education programs	■ Establish benchmarks for ensuring school counseling students graduate with the knowledge, attitudes and skills needed for developing comprehensive school counseling programs

The school counselor competencies assessment on p. 148 helps school counselors assess their knowledge, attitudes and skills.

SCHOOL COUNSELING PROGRAM ASSESSMENT

The school counseling program assessment is used to self-evaluate the school counseling program in comparison with the ASCA National Model. The assessment findings help school counselors identify strengths and weaknesses of the school counseling program and provide direction for continued program improvement.

The assessment is first completed when a comprehensive school counseling program is being designed and then reviewed and updated at least annually to appraise the progress of program development and implementation. After completing the assessment, see p. 105 in the accountability section for more information about analyzing the data to determine:
■ Major strengths of the program
■ Program areas in need of strengthening
■ Short-range goals for improvement
■ Long-range goals for improvement
■ Areas to consider for professional development

Results of the assessment can be shared in several ways to support the development of a comprehensive program. The results can be shared with administrators to inform the administrator of the direction of program implementation. The results may also be shared with the advisory council to inform the development of program priorities and goals, training and areas of focus.

See p. 59 for the school counseling program assessment.

USE-OF-TIME ASSESSMENT

The use-of-time assessment helps the school counselor determine how much time is spent in each of the components of the ASCA National Model. School counselors with comprehensive school counseling programs spend a majority of their time providing direct and indirect services to students. It is recommended that school counselors complete the use-of-time assessment twice a year.

- **Direct student services** are in-person interactions between school counselors and students. Through the direct services components of school counseling core curriculum, individual student planning and responsive services, school counselors help students develop the knowledge, attitudes and skills identified from the school counseling core curriculum.

- **Indirect student services** are services provided on behalf of students as a result of the school counselor's interactions with others. Through indirect services, school counselors provide leadership, advocacy and collaboration, which enhance student achievement and promote systemic change related to equity and access.

See p. 84 and 87 of the Delivery section for more information about direct and indirect services.

It is recommended that school counselors spend 80 percent or more of their time in direct student services and indirect student services. The remaining 20 percent of time is set aside for program management and school support services, such as school counseling program foundation, management and accountability tasks. In addition, a small portion of the 20 percent of the school counselor's time is spent in fair-share responsibilities – the "routine 'running of the school' responsibilities that all members of the school staff take equal turns doing to ensure the school's smooth operation" (Gysbers & Henderson, 2012, p. 83).

Although spending 80 percent of time in direct and indirect student services is the general recommendation for a comprehensive school counseling program, use of time within the 80 percent may be allocated differently from school to school based on needs identified in school data. Although all components of direct and indirect student services are necessary for a program to be considered a comprehensive school counseling program, decisions about time allocation are based on student needs as demonstrated in the school data profile (p. 66) and alignment with school and school counseling program goals.

School counselors may find it necessary to adjust the percentage of time in each of the delivery categories from year to year to meet students' needs. In addition, school counselors are able to justify their modification to the suggested use of time by providing a rationale for an increase or decrease to any category based on research and best practice. In programs with more than one school counselor per site, there is often flexibility between and among school counselors in determining how much time individual school counselors spend in the delivery components.

The use-of-time assessment (p. 63) helps school counselors determine how they are currently using their time and can assist in drawing conclusions about how much time is currently being spent on school counseling activities versus non-school-counseling activities. The accountability section of the ASCA National Model provides further information on the analysis of data collected through this assessment.

Delivery is 80% or more of the activity in the ASCA National Model

Delivery

Accountability

Management

Foundation

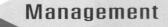

80%

Use of Time: Appropriate and Inappropriate School Counseling Activities

School counselors' duties are focused on the overall delivery of the comprehensive school counseling program – direct and indirect student services and program management and school support. Administrators are encouraged to eliminate or reassign inappropriate tasks, allowing school counselors to focus on the prevention and intervention needs of their program. The chart below represents a comparison between the two similar types of activities and serves as a helpful teaching tool when explaining school counseling program activities.

Appropriate Activities for School Counselors	*Inappropriate Activities for School Counselors*
■ individual student academic program planning	■ coordinating paperwork and data entry of all new students
■ interpreting cognitive, aptitude and achievement tests	■ coordinating cognitive, aptitude and achievement testing programs
■ providing counseling to students who are tardy or absent	■ signing excuses for students who are tardy or absent
■ providing counseling to students who have disciplinary problems	■ performing disciplinary actions or assigning discipline consequences
■ providing counseling to students as to appropriate school dress	■ sending students home who are not appropriately dressed
■ collaborating with teachers to present school counseling core curriculum lessons	■ teaching classes when teachers are absent
■ analyzing grade-point averages in relationship to achievement	■ computing grade-point averages
■ interpreting student records	■ maintaining student records
■ providing teachers with suggestions for effective classroom management	■ supervising classrooms or common areas
■ ensuring student records are maintained as per state and federal regulations	■ keeping clerical records
■ helping the school principal identify and resolve student issues, needs and problems	■ assisting with duties in the principal's office
■ providing individual and small-group counseling services to students	■ providing therapy or long-term counseling in schools to address psychological disorders (see Responsive Services on p. 86 for more detailed information on therapy)
■ advocating for students at individual education plan meetings, student study teams and school attendance review boards	■ coordinating schoolwide individual education plans, student study teams and school attendance review boards
■ analyzing disaggregated data	■ serving as a data entry clerk

Adapted from Campbell, C.A. & Dahir, C.A. (1997) *Sharing the vision: The ASCA national standards for school counseling programs*, Alexandria, VA: American School Counselor Association.

ANNUAL AGREEMENT

Annual agreements outline the organization and focus of the school counseling program and are made between each school counselor and the administrator in charge of the school counseling program each school year. These agreements ensure formal discussion between the school counselor and administrator about the alignment of school counseling program goals with the goals of the school and can increase an administrator's understanding of a comprehensive school counseling program. Each school counselor develops an annual agreement with the administrator.

When developing the agreement, it is recommended that the agreement:
- Is created and signed by the school counselor and supervising administrator within the first two months of school
- Provides rationale for the school counselor's use of time based on the school's data
- Reflects the school counseling program's mission and program goals, which align with the school's mission
- Lists the school counselor's specific responsibilities within the school counseling program, such as student caseload and program components or activities
- Identifies areas for professional development for the school counselor

When school counselors and administrators meet and agree on program priorities, implementation strategies and the organization of the school counseling program, the program runs more smoothly and is more likely to produce the desired results for students.

Suggested Steps for Developing an Effective Annual Agreement
1. Review the annual agreement template as a school counseling team, if appropriate, as early in the year as possible to discuss areas of information needed
2. Determine any sections of the agreement that will be the same for all school counselors in the building, if appropriate
3. Complete the annual agreement template within the first month of school (one per school counselor)
4. Schedule an appointment to meet with the principal to review the agreement
5. Provide a quick but thorough overview of program goals and priorities when meeting with the principal, using the completed annual agreement to guide the conversation
6. Consider feedback from the principal, and adjust agreement as needed
7. Collect signatures of school counselor(s) and principal before the end of the second month of school

Non-School-Counseling Duties
Non-school-counseling duties take away valuable time from implementing a school counseling program that meets the needs of all students. Consider these steps for the reassignment of non-school-counseling duties.

1. Identify tasks school counselors are currently responsible for that do not align with the appropriate duties of a school counselor (see appropriate and inappropriate activities for school counselors in the Use of Time section, p. 43).

2. Use data from the use-of-time assessment or estimate the amount of time in hours these duties take away from implementation of the school counseling program.
3. Consider if the tasks really need to be completed and how else the tasks might be completed, including through use of technology for increased efficiency.
4. Determine what school counseling activities would replace these tasks if they were removed, and estimate the impact on students.
5. Express willingness to be a part of a plan for successful transfer of the tasks to staff who have skills to complete the task, keeping in mind that other staff members may already have a large list of responsibilities as well.
6. Recognize that reassigning tasks may take time.

Adapted from Gysbers, N.C. & Henderson, P. (2012) *Developing and managing your school counseling program* (5th ed.), Alexandria, VA: American Counseling Association.

ADVISORY COUNCIL

An advisory council is a representative group of stakeholders selected to review and advise on the implementation of the school counseling program. The council meets at least twice a year and maintains an agenda and minutes for each meeting.

Advisory councils assist school counselors by:
- Advising on program goals
- Reviewing program results
- Making recommendations about the school counseling program
- Advocating and engaging in public relations for the school counseling program
- Advocating for funding and resources

(Johnson & Johnson, 2001)

Creating an Advisory Council
When creating an advisory council, school counselors consider items such as:

- Goals and objectives – The advisory council's goals and objectives are set in advance of selecting advisory council members. School counselors are responsible for helping the members understand the council's purpose and focus. Council members can provide feedback on the goals and objectives, which can be revised as needed.

- Representation – The broader the representation on the advisory council, the more the group's work will accurately reflect the community's values, concerns and interests. Ideally, members of the advisory council reflect the diversity of the community and include students, parents, teachers, school counselors, administrators, school board members, and business and community members.

- Size – Although broad representation is crucial, the council's size is an important issue. It is important to create an environment that encourages informed, constructive discussion. A council with too many members may be ineffective. Generally, a good rule of thumb is to establish a council with a minimum of eight members and a maximum of 20 members.

- Appropriate candidates – Advisory councils function as a communications link between the school counseling program and the various groups in the school and community: students, parents or guardians, educators, businesses and the community organizations. Appointing members with sincere interest in the school counseling program is recommended. Officially invite potential members by letter to serve on the advisory council, and provide a brief explanation of the purpose of the council and the amount of time that may be needed. Also give potential members an opportunity to decline.

- Chairperson – An effective advisory council chairperson has skills in planning and conducting meetings. Additionally, the chairperson should possess group facilitation skills and consistently demonstrate an effective working relationships with others.

- Terms of membership – Terms of membership include appointments to definite terms of office serving from one to three years. If terms are staggered, there will always be experienced members serving. When a member's term has expired, appoint a new council member for a new term.

- Agenda and minutes – To ensure effectiveness, it is important that each advisory council meeting have a specific agenda and goals to be accomplished. Send minutes of previous meetings and an agenda of the upcoming meeting to each member several days in advance.

- First meeting – The chairperson calls the first meeting of the council. Detailed information is provided to council members to inform members of the council's purpose and goals. In addition, reports, school data and other information previously collected are included in an information packet to each member. Setting meeting dates and times and other organizational activities should take place at the first meeting. Although the number of meetings may vary, the school counseling advisory council should meet at least twice a year to collaborate and provide input.

- Additional meetings – As the group forms and develops an identity, agenda topics may naturally arise. However, part of the focus for the first meeting of the school year may be presenting the school counseling program calendar, goals and objectives. At the end of the year, the results gained in the program during the year can be shared along with recommendations for program improvement.

USE OF DATA

The focus and direction of the comprehensive school counseling program is based on student needs as determined through a review of the school's data. Understanding and using data are essential to ensuring equitable services and that every student receives the benefits of the school counseling program.

School counselors show activities implemented as part of the school counseling program were developed after a careful analysis of achievement, attendance and behavioral data.

The use of data helps school counselors:

- Monitor student progress
- Identify students who are having difficulties or behavior problems
- Identify barriers to learning
- Understand factors affecting student behavior
- Identify access and equity issues
- Close achievement, opportunity and attainment gaps
- Assess and evaluate the effectiveness of activities within the school counseling program
- Improve, modify or change services provided to students
- Educate stakeholders about the power of a comprehensive school counseling program
- Advocate for additional resources to increase program effectiveness

A comprehensive school counseling program requires school counselors to be proficient in the collection, analysis and interpretation of student achievement, attendance and behavioral data. While the management component of the ASCA National Model aids school counselors by providing tools for planning and data collection, the accountability component helps with data analysis and program results.

Disaggregating Data

To ensure every student achieves high academic standards, it is important to understand aggregate, global data from the entire student body, but it is even more important to understand the disaggregated data. When disaggregating data, school counselors separate data by variables to determine if there are any groups of students who are not performing as well as others.

For example, a school counselor may be pleased with data revealing that 85 percent of all seniors attend post-secondary education but not be as pleased if disaggregated data reveal that 93 percent of white students attend post-secondary education compared with only 42 percent of students of color. Disaggregated data often brings to light issues of equity and access and helps focus the discussion upon the needs of specific groups of students.

Although there are many ways to disaggregate data, frequently used categories include:

- Gender
- Race/ethnicity
- Socio-economic status* (free or reduced lunch)
- Course enrollment
- Language spoken at home
- Special education
- Grade level
- Teacher assignment

*Although the socio-economic status of individual students may be helpful in understanding student backgrounds, these data are protected by federal and state laws and may not be available to school counselors. Making decisions about prevention or intervention activities based on academic, attendance and behavioral data will help school counselors meet the needs of any student, regardless of background, who is not achieving success.

SCHOOL DATA PROFILE

Using student and school site data to monitor student progress helps the school counselor determine what students need to achieve school success. The school data profile template can be used to help school counselors organize and disaggregate data, particularly if the school's student information system does not produce reports in a disaggregated format. Disaggregated data are needed for the school counselor to gain an understanding of whether or not achievement gaps or issues of equity exist at the school. The following types of data can help school counselors better understand the needs of all students.

Achievement Data
Achievement data measure students' academic progress. Achievement data fields include:
- Promotion and retention rates
- Graduation rates
- Drop-out rates
- Standardized test data (e.g., state exams, SAT/ACT scores)
- Grade-point averages
- At or above grade/achievement level in reading, math, etc.
- Passing all classes
- Completion of specific academic programs (e.g., academic honors, college prep, etc.)

Behavioral Data
Behavioral data measure those fields the literature has shown to be correlated to academic achievement. These data fields include:
- Discipline referrals
- Suspension rates
- Alcohol, tobacco and other drug violations
- Attendance rates
- Course enrollment patterns
- Post-secondary education attendance rates
- Parent or guardian involvement
- Participation in extracurricular activities
- Homework completion rates

The school data profile (see p. 66) is provided as a template framework for documenting current school data as well as data over time. Collecting data over time can help provide a better understanding of the impact of the school counseling program. Data are collected in short-term and long-term formats.

Short term: Data that measure the short-term impact of changes in knowledge, attitudes and skills as a result of school counseling activities or interventions such as:
- Pre-post tests on student competencies addressed in a classroom unit
- Four-year/graduation plans
- Improved test scores after delivering test-taking lessons
- Improved classroom behavior after small-group counseling
- Improved grades from one quarter to another after delivering homework or study skill lessons.

Long term: Schoolwide year-to-year, longitudinal student impact data collected for areas such as:
- Promotion and graduation rates
- Attendance rates
- Suspension rates
- College acceptance rates

PROGRAM RESULTS DATA

School counselors use data not only to identify areas of concern but also to show the school counseling program has attained goals and made a difference for students (Dimmitt, Carey & Hatch, 2007). To document how students are different as a result of the school counseling program, school counselors collect and analyze process, perception and outcome data and include them in program activity results reports.

Process data: Process data answer the question, "What did you do for whom?" and provide evidence that an event occurred. These data describe the way the activities are conducted and how many students were affected by the activity.

Examples of Process Data	<ul><li>Eight fourth-grade students participated in a study skills group that met six times for 45 minutes</li><li>450 ninth-graders completed an individual learning plan</li><li>38 parents attended the middle school orientation meeting</li></ul>

Perception data: Perception data answer the question, "What do people think they know, believe or can do?" These data can be collected through surveys such as pre-post tests, needs assessments, program evaluation surveys or feedback surveys measuring self-reports of:
- Attainment of competencies
- Changes in attitudes and beliefs
- Perceived gains in knowledge

The following types of surveys may be used to inform the school counseling program.

Pre-Post	Given before and after an intervention to determine knowledge gained or to measure a change in perspective
Needs Assessment	Given to students or stakeholders to gather their perception of student or program needs
Program/Activity Evaluation	Given after an intervention or activity to gather participants' opinions about the value of the intervention or activity
Opinion Survey	Given to students or stakeholders to understand their perceptions of the school counseling program or activities

Examples of perception data include:

Competencies Attainment	■ 100 percent of ninth-graders understand graduation requirements and have completed a graduation plan ■ 100 percent of sixth-graders can identify three career interests
Changes in Attitudes or Beliefs	■ 93 percent of fourth-graders believe fighting is not an appropriate method of solving problems ■ 69 percent of all students report feeling safe at school ■ 90 percent of the parents report benefiting from a presentation on college entrance requirements
Gains in Knowledge	■ 89 percent of ninth-graders demonstrate knowledge of promotion requirements ■ 92 percent of all students can identify the early warning signs of violence

Outcome data: Although it is important to keep track of process and perception data so interventions can be replicated or improved, these data alone are not sufficient to evaluate the effectiveness of interventions. Outcome data show the impact of an activity or program and answer the question, "So what?"

Outcome data provide data provide school counselors with the opportunity to discuss the extent to which the program has had a positive impact on students' ability to utilize their knowledge, attitudes and skills to effect improvement in achievement and behavior. These data are collected from multiple sources and include fields such as promotion rates, attendance rates, number of discipline referrals, grade-point averages, student graduation rates, etc. Examples of outcome data for behavior change include:

Achievement Outcome Data	■ Graduation rate improved from 79 percent to 86 percent. ■ Identified ninth-graders increased GPA from 2.0 to 3.4 between first and final marking period. ■ Fourth-graders improved state math score from 69 to 73.
Attendance Outcome Data	■ Average attendance increased from 88 percent to 91 percent. ■ Identified students decreased average number of days absent from 15 to 8 during final marking period.
Behavioral Outcome Data	■ Discipline referrals decreased by 30 percent for students with four or more referrals. ■ Number of students referred for discipline decreased by 15 percent by the end of the school year.

Most of the data fields mentioned above are typically available in the school's student information system. These systems or databases greatly enhance the school counselor's ability to monitor every student's progress and help to make these formerly daunting tasks a manageable and valuable strategy.

Although data collection and analysis are important, school counselors do not have the time or resources to monitor every activity within the school counseling program. Therefore choices are made based on school priorities and data available at the local site. School and district goals, school improvement plans and other documents will help the school counselor determine what activities may be the highest priority. Each school district should provide direction on what is most important to be monitored.

Although collecting and analyzing data are important, these activities do not imply that school counselors are data analysts or attendance clerks. Schools may ask administrators or data managers to assist in the collection and management of this information, or they may hire para-professionals to assist with these tasks. Although data collection and analyses take time, the benefits for students and the school counseling program greatly outweigh these costs.

ACTION PLANS

To efficiently and effectively deliver the school counseling program, there must be a plan detailing how the school counselor intends to achieve the desired results (Johnson & Johnson, 2001). Action plans are utilized within three areas: school counseling curriculum, small groups and closing-the-gap activities.

The templates of all three types of action plan are similar and contain the following information:
- Goals to be addressed
- Domain(s), standard(s) and competencies, which are consistent with school and program goals
- Description of school counseling activities to be delivered
- Title of any packaged or created curriculum that will be used
- Timeline for completion of activities
- Name of person(s) responsible for each activity
- Methods of evaluating school success using process, perception and outcome data
- Expected results for students stated in terms of what will be demonstrated by the student

Curriculum Action Plan
Delivering school counseling curriculum activities can be an effective way to increase student achievement and improve student behaviors and attitudes (Whiston & Quinby, 2009). The curriculum action plan template helps school counselors create an effective plan to help students develop the knowledge, attitudes and skills appropriate for their developmental level within the domains of academic, career and personal/social development.

School counseling curriculum activities are presented systematically in the school (preK-12) through classroom and group activities. The template (see p. 69) assists school counselors in the design, documentation and implementation of the school counseling curriculum.

- Design – School counselors design the curriculum by selecting specific competencies that address student needs as demonstrated through school data. The competencies are selected from, or align with, the ASCA Student Standards. Lessons are selected or created to help students gain the appropriate knowledge, attitudes or skills specified in the plan.
- Documentation – The curriculum is documented through the school counseling core curriculum action plan. The plan includes the lessons taught, competencies addressed, curriculum used, timelines, projected students, evaluation methods and persons responsible.
- Implementation – The curriculum is implemented through direct instruction, team teaching or coordination with other educators. The competencies are taught using a variety of curriculum materials or activities. Student attainment of the competencies is assessed using pre-post tests, product creation or activity completion.

Small-Group Action Plan

Small-group activities have also been shown to have a positive effect on student achievement and behavior (Whiston & Quinby, 2009). The small-group action plan template (see p. 70) is used to provide focus and organization to the academic, attendance or behavioral goals of small-group counseling activities.

Like individual counseling, small-group counseling is provided as a short-term intervention and typically involves four to eight sessions organized to meet specific prevention or intervention goals. The template assists school counselors in the design, documentation and implementation of small groups.

- Design – School counselors select students for small groups based on academic, behavior or attendance needs as reflected in school data. Specific competencies addressing student needs are selected from, or align with, the ASCA Student Standards. Lessons or activities are selected or created to help students gain the appropriate knowledge, attitudes or skills specified in the plan.
- Documentation – The small group is documented through the small-group action plan. The plan includes the lessons and activities, competencies addressed, curriculum used, timelines, projected students, evaluation methods and persons responsible.
- Implementation – The small group is implemented using counseling skills and techniques appropriate for the group and a variety of curriculum materials or activities. Student attainment of the competencies is assessed using pre-post tests and success toward reaching the established goals of the group.

Closing-the-Gap Action Plan

The closing-the-gap action plan template serves as a guide to address academic or behavioral discrepancies that exist between student groups. These discrepancies, often referred to as gaps, are identified through the review of disaggregated data, and school counselors develop detailed action plans indicating activities and resources leveraged to close the gaps.

Closing-the-gap activities often change from year to year based on student needs as demonstrated in the school's data. The template (see p. 71) assists school counselors in the design, implementation and documentation of closing-the-gap action plans.

- Design – School counselors identify students for closing-the-gap activities based on academic, attendance and behavior needs as reflected in school data. Specific competencies addressing student needs are selected from, or align with, the ASCA Student Standards. Activities and interventions are selected or created to help students meet the goals specified in the plan.
- Documentation – The activities and interventions are documented through the closing-the-gap action plan. The plan includes the activities and interventions, competencies addressed, curriculum used, timelines, projected students, evaluation methods and persons responsible.
- Implementation – The activities and interventions are implemented using counseling, collaboration, advocacy and referral skills appropriate for the identified students. Student attainment of the competencies is assessed using pre-post tests and improvement in achievement, attendance or behavior as specified in the plan.

LESSON PLANS

To successfully deliver classroom lessons related to the school counseling core curriculum, the importance of lesson planning cannot be overstated. School counselors have limited time to spend in classrooms, and it is imperative to give enough time and thought about what will be delivered, to whom it will be delivered, how it will be delivered and how student attainment of the competencies will be evaluated.

The lesson plan template (see p. 72) can help school counselors plan an effective classroom or large-group lesson. Lesson plan topics include:

- **ASCA Student Standards** – Identify the appropriate domain, standard and competencies from the ASCA Student Standards. The selected standard and competency guide the lesson content.
- **Learning objectives** – State a clear, measurable learning objective related to the selected competency. Verb lists from the revised Bloom's Taxonomy (Krathwohl, 2002) may be helpful in writing measurable learning objectives; search online to find the list.
- **Materials** – List any materials needed to deliver the lesson.
- **Procedure** – Include steps to:
  - Introduce the lesson
  - Present the content
  - Check for understanding during the lesson by using simple assessments such as think-pair-share (Jones, Jones & Vermette, 2011)
- **Plan for evaluation** – Determine how you will collect process, perception and outcome data.
  - *Process data* – Identify the number of students who will participate.
  - *Perception data* – Allowing students time to create a tangible product that matches the learning objective during class is an active and visible assessment of whether or not the students attained the competency and learning objective (Jones, et al., 2011). In addition, pre- and post-tests will provide perception data.

- *Outcome data* – Identify what academic, attendance or behavioral data the lesson is designed to affect. Although it is unlikely one lesson will have a strong impact on outcome data, a full curriculum or series of lessons on a topic may have a more significant impact.

  Although it is impractical to collect outcome data on every lesson presented, collect all three types of data on several lessons each year to measure the extent to which the lesson has had a positive impact on student outcomes.

- **Follow up** – If the lesson is important enough to teach, it is important that all students master the competency and learning objective. Plan for how you will follow up with any students who do not master the competencies of the lesson (DuFour, Eaker, Karhanek, and DuFour, 2004).

CALENDARS

School counselors develop and publish calendars of school counseling events to inform students, parents, teachers and administrators of what, when and where school counseling activities will be held. Creating calendars also assists school counselors with the development of a comprehensive school counseling program that provides activities and services for all students in the school.

Publicizing the school counseling program calendar encourages staff, parent, student and community involvement as partners in student education. As the program grows and multiple activities are developed, a calendar validates the important support the school counselor program provides students, parents or guardians, teachers and administrators.

A well-developed calendar that is complete, timely and visually appealing can be a powerful public relations booster. Time and thought in the following areas can help to produce a useful tool:
- Format for ease of understanding
- Consistency in timing and distribution methods (weekly, monthly, annually)
- Attractiveness of the design, color and detail
- Identification of grade levels, dates and activities
- Distribution to appropriate persons: students, staff, parents or guardians and community
- Comparison with established goals for time spent in the elements and strategies of the delivery

(Gysbers & Henderson, 2012; Johnson & Johnson, 2001; Myrick, 2003).

Annual calendar
School counselors use the annual calendar to identify and communicate school counseling program priorities. The school counseling program has one annual calendar that includes all major school counseling activities delivered or coordinated by the school counselor(s). The annual calendar can increase visibility of the school counseling program and provide focus on events or activities of value for the students, parents and staff.

The annual calendar includes activities such as:
- school counseling classroom lessons
- back-to-school night
- open house
- student/parent/teacher meeting days
- standardized tests dates
- career or college nights
- evening activities provided through the school and the community

Organizing the annual calendar in a monthly format can be useful in reminding students, teachers, parents and administrators about upcoming events. The current or upcoming month's events can be posted in prominent places such as the school's Web site, department and classroom bulletin boards, administrative offices, career center and other sites used to communicate school events. It may also be submitted to the student newspaper or the local newspaper to increase the program's visibility.

Weekly calendars
Each school counselor creates a weekly calendar that provides a detailed plan of the school counselor's activities for the week. Although the weekly calendar is somewhat flexible due to crisis or immediate student needs that may occur unexpectedly, this calendar serves as a plan for program implementation on a daily basis. The weekly calendar includes activities such as:
- classroom lessons
- group and individual counseling
- meetings with students
- collaboration and advocacy
- data analysis
- committee and fair-share responsibilities

References

American School Counselor Association (2007). *School counselor competencies.* Alexandria, VA: Author.

Campbell, C. A. & Dahir, C. A. (1997). *Sharing the vision: The national standards for school counseling programs.* Alexandria, VA: American School Counselor Association.

Dimmitt, C., Carey, J., & Hatch, T. (2007). *Evidence-based school counseling: Making a difference with data-driven practices.* Thousand Oaks, CA: Corwin Press.

DuFour, R., Eaker, R., Karhanek, G., and DuFour, R., (2004). *Whatever it takes: How professional learning communities respond when students don't learn.* Bloomington: Solution Tree.

Gysbers, N. C. & Henderson, P. (2012) *Developing and managing your school counseling program* (5th ed.), Alexandria, VA: American Counseling Association.

Johnson, C. D. & Johnson, S. K. (2001) *Results-based student support programs: Leadership academy workbook.* San Juan Capistrano, CA: Professional Update.

Jones, K. A., Jones, J., and Vermette, P. J. (2011). Six common lesson planning pitfalls: Recommendations for novice educators. *Education, 131*(4), 845-64.

Krathwohl, D. R. (2002). A Revision of Bloom's Taxonomy: An Overview. *Theory into Practice, 41*(4), 213-218.

Myrick, R. D. (2003). *Developmental guidance and counseling: A practical approach* (4th ed.). Minneapolis, MN: Educational Media Corporation.

Whiston, S. C. & Quinby, R. F. (2009). Review of school counseling outcome research. *Psychology in the Schools, 46*(3), 267-272.

SCHOOL COUNSELING PROGRAM ASSESSMENT

FOUNDATION			
CRITERIA	No	In Progress	Yes
Beliefs			
a. Indicates an agreed-upon belief system about the ability of all students to achieve			
b. Addresses how the school counseling program meets student developmental needs			
c. Addresses the school counselor's role as an advocate for every students			
d. Identifies persons to be involved in the planning, managing, delivery and evaluation of school counseling program activities			
e. Includes how data informs program decisions			
f. Includes how ethical standards guide the work of school counselors			
Vision Statement			
a. Describes a future where school counseling goals and strategies are being successfully achieved			
b. Outlines a rich and textual picture of what success looks like and feels like			
c. Is bold and inspiring			
d. States best possible student outcomes			
e. Is believable and achievable			
Mission Statement			
a. Aligns with the school's mission statement and may show linkages to district and state department of education mission statements			
b. Written with students as the primary focus			
c. Advocates for equity, access and success of every student			
d. Indicates the long-range results desired for all students			
Program Goals			
a. Promote achievement, attendance, behavior and/or school safety			
b. Are based on school data			
c. Address schoolwide data, policies and practices or address closing-the-gap issues			
d. Address academic, career and/or personal/social development			

FOUNDATION, cont.

CRITERIA	No	In Progress	Yes
ASCA Student Standards and Other Student Standards			
a. Standards, competencies and indicators from ASCA Student Standards are identified and align with program mission and goals			
b. Standards and competencies selected from other student standards (state/district, 21st Century, Character Ed, etc.) align with ASCA Student Standards, program mission and goals as appropriate			
School Counselor Professional Competencies and Ethical Standards			
a. ASCA School Counselor Competencies have been reviewed			
b. ASCA Ethical Standards for School Counselors have been reviewed			

PROGRAM MANAGEMENT

CRITERIA	No	In Progress	Yes
School Counselor Competencies Assessment			
School counselor competencies assessment has been completed			
School Counseling Program Assessment			
School counseling program assessment has been completed			
Use-of-Time Assessment			
a. Use-of-time assessment completed twice a year			
b. Direct and indirect services account for 80 percent of time or more			
c. Program management and school support activities account for 20 percent of time or less			
Annual Agreement			
a. Created and signed by the school counselor and supervising administrator within the first two months of school			
b. One agreement per school counselor			
c. Provides rationale for use of time based on data and goals			
d. Reflects school counseling program mission and program goals			
e. Lists school counselor roles and responsibilities			
f. Identifies areas for school counselor professional development			

PROGRAM MANAGEMENT, cont.

CRITERIA	No	In Progress	Yes
Advisory Council			
a. Membership includes administrator and representatives of school and community stakeholders			
b. Meets at least twice a year and maintains agenda and minutes			
c. Advises on school counseling program goals, reviews program results and makes recommendations			
d. Advocates and engages in public relations for the school counseling program			
e. Advocates for school counseling program funding and resources			
Use of Data			
a. School data profile completed, tracking achievement, attendance, behavior and safety data			
b. School data inform program goals			
c. School counseling program data (process, perception, outcome) are collected and reviewed and inform program decisions			
d. Organizes and shares data/results in a user-friendly format (e.g., charts)			
Action Plans (Curriculum, Small Group and Closing the Gap)			
a. Data are used to develop curriculum, small-group and closing-the-gap action plans using action plan templates			
b. Action plans are consistent with the program goals and competencies			
c. Projected results (process, perception and outcome) data have been identified			
d. Projected outcome data are stated in terms of what the student will demonstrate			
Curriculum Lesson Plan			
Curriculum lesson plan templates are used to develop and implement classroom activities			
Calendars (Annual and Weekly)			
a. Indicate activities of a comprehensive school counseling program			
b. Reflect program goals and activities of school counseling curriculum, small-group and closing-the-gap action plans			
c. Are published and distributed to appropriate persons			
d. Indicate fair-share responsibilities			
e. Weekly calendar aligns with planned use of time in the annual agreement			

DELIVERY			
CRITERIA	No	In Progress	Yes
Direct student services are provided (Strategies to include instruction, group activities, appraisal, advisement, counseling and crisis response)			
a. Deliver school counseling curriculum lessons to classroom and large groups			
b. Provide appraisal and advisement to assist all students with academic, career and personal/social planning			
c. Provide individual and/or group counseling to identified students with identified concerns or needs			
Indirect student services are provided to identified students (Strategies to include referrals, consultation, collaboration)			
Direct and indirect service provision amounts to 80 percent or more of the school counselor's time			

ACCOUNTABILITY			
CRITERIA	No	In Progress	Yes
Data Tracking			
a. School data profile is analyzed, and implications for results over time are considered			
b. Use-of-time assessment is analyzed and implications are considered			
Program Results (Process, Perception and Outcome Data)			
a. Curriculum results report is analyzed, and implications are considered			
b. Small-group results reports are analyzed, and implications are considered			
c. Closing-the-gap results reports are analyzed, and implications are considered			
d. Program results are shared with stakeholders			
Evaluation and Improvement			
a. School counselor competencies assessment informs self-improvement and professional development			
b. School counseling program assessment informs program improvement			
c. School counselor performance appraisal is conducted and informs improvement			
d. Program goal results are analyzed, and implications considered			

USE-OF-TIME ASSESSMENT

	Direct Student Services			Indirect Student Services	Program Management and School Support		Non-School-Counseling Tasks
	School Counseling Core Curriculum	Individual Student Planning	Responsive Services	Referrals/ Consultation/ Collaboration	Program Foundation, Management and Accountability	Fair-Share Responsibility	Non-School-Counseling Tasks
7-7:15 a.m.							
7:16-7:30 a.m.							
7:31-7:45 a.m.							
7:46-8 a.m.							
8:01-8:15 a.m.							
8:16-8:30 a.m.							
8:31-8:45 a.m.							
8:46-9 a.m.							
9:01-9:15 a.m.							
9:16-9:30 a.m.							
9:31-9:45 a.m.							
9:46-10 a.m.							
10:01-10:15 a.m.							
10:16-10:30 a.m.							
10:31-10:45							
10:46-11 a.m.							
11:01-11:15 a.m.							
11:16-11:30 a.m.							
11:31-11:45 a.m.							
11:45 a.m.-12 p.m.							
12:01-12:15 p.m.							
12:16-12:30 p.m.							
12:31-12:45							
12:46-1 p.m.							
1:01-1:15 p.m.							
1:16-1:30 p.m.							
1:31-1:45 p.m.							
1:46-2 p.m.							
2:01-2:15 p.m.							
2:16-2:30 p.m.							
2:31-2:45 p.m.							
2:46-3 p.m.							
3:01-3:15 p.m.							
3:16-3:30 p.m.							
3:31-3:45 p.m.							
3:46-4 p.m.							
TOTALS							
% per topic							
% per category							

ANNUAL AGREEMENT TEMPLATE

School Counselor_____ Year _____

School Counseling Program Mission Statement

_____

School Counseling Program Goals

The school counseling program will focus on the following achievement, attendance, behavior and/or school safety goals this year. Details of activities promoting these goals are found in the curriculum, small-group and closing-the-gap action plans.

Program Goal Statements	
1	
2	
3	

Use of Time

I plan to spend the following percentage of my time delivering the components of the school counseling program. All components are required for a comprehensive school counseling program.

	Planned Use			Suggested
Direct Services to Students	_____%	of time delivering school counseling core curriculum	Provides developmental curriculum content in a systematic way to all students	80% or more
	_____%	of time with individual student planning	Assists students in the development of educational, career and personal plans	
	_____%	of time with responsive services	Addresses the immediate concerns of students	
Indirect Services for Students	_____%	of time providing referrals, consultation and collaboration	Interacts with others to provide support for student achievement	
Program Planning and School Support	_____%	of time with foundation, management and accountability and school support	Includes planning and evaluating the school counseling program and school support activities	20% or less

Professional Development

I plan to participate in the following professional development based on school counseling program goals and my school counselor competencies self-assessment.

_____

ANNUAL AGREEMENT, cont.

School Counselor Responsibilities

My specific responsibilities include:

Caseload _____ Number of students in caseload _____

School Counseling Program Components/Activities: _____

_____

Other Responsibilities: _____

Advisory Council

The school counseling advisory council will meet on the following dates.

_____

Planning and Results Documents

The following documents have been developed for the school counseling program.

☐ Annual Calendar   ☐ Closing-the-Gap Action Plans
☐ Curriculum Action Plan   ☐ Results Reports (from last year's action plans)
☐ Small-Group Action Plan

Professional Collaboration and Responsibilities Choose all that apply.

Group	Weekly/Monthly	Coordinator
A. School Counseling Team Meetings		
B. Administration/School Counseling Meetings		
C. Student Support Team Meetings		
D. Department Chair Meetings		
E. School Improvement Team Meetings		
F. District School Counseling Meetings		
G. (Other)		

Budget Materials and Supplies

Annual Budget $_____ Materials and supplies needed:

_____

School Counselor Availability/Office Organization

The school counseling office will be open for students/parents/teachers from _____to_____
My hours will be from _____to_____ (if flexible scheduling is used)
The career center will be open from _____to_____

Role and Responsibilities of Other Staff and Volunteers

School Counseling Department Assistant _____

Attendance Assistant Clerk_____

Data Manager/Registrar _____

Career and College Center Assistant _____

Other Staff _____

Volunteers_____

_____
School Counselor Signature   Principal Signature   Date

SCHOOL DATA PROFILE TEMPLATE

School Data Profile

School Year	#	%	#	%	#	%
Enrollment	#	%	#	%	#	%
Total enrollment						
Gifted (school-based)						
ESOL						
Special education services						

School Year						
Dropout Rate	%		%		%	
All students						
Asian or Pacific Islander						
Black						
Hispanic/Latino						
White						
Students with disabilities						
Students identified as disadvantaged						
Limited-English-proficiency students						
Graduation or Promotion Rate	%		%		%	
All students						
Asian or Pacific Islander						
Black						
Hispanic/Latino						
White						
Students with disabilities						
Students identified as disadvantaged						
Limited-English-proficiency students						

School Year						
Attendance	%		%		%	
All Students						
Asian or Pacific Islander						
Black						
Hispanic/Latino						
White						
Students with disabilities						
Students identified as disadvantaged						
Limited-English-proficiency students						

School Data Profile, cont.

Students with Disabilities	#	%	#	%	#	%
School Year						
All Students with disabilities						
Asian or Pacific Islander						
Black						
Hispanic/Latino						
White						
Other						

School Safety	#	%	#	%	#	%
School Year						
Weapons offenses						
Offenses against students						
Offenses against staff						
Alcohol, tobacco, drug offenses						
Disorderly or disruptive behavior						
Technology offenses						

Engagement Data	#	%	#	%	#	%
School Year						
Students in rigorous courses						
Students graduating without retention						
Students in extracurricular activities						
Student detentions						
Student suspensions						

Achievement	#	%	#	%	#	%
School Year						
All students with disabilities						
Asian or Pacific Islander						
Black						
Hispanic/Latino						
White						
Other						

School Data Profile, cont.

School Year	#	%	#	%	#	%
Achievement						
All students with disabilities						
Asian or Pacific Islander						
Black						
Hispanic/Latino						
White						
Other						

School Year	#	%	#	%	#	%
Achievement						
All students						
Asian or Pacific Islander						
Black						
Hispanic/Latino						
White						
Other						

School Year	#	%	#	%	#	%
Achievement						
All students						
Asian or Pacific Islander						
Black						
Hispanic/Latino						
White						
Other						

School Year	#	%	#	%	#	%
Achievement						
All students						
Asian or Pacific Islander						
Black						
Hispanic/Latino						
White						
Other						

SCHOOL COUNSELING CORE CURRICULUM ACTION PLAN

Year: _____

Goal: _____

Lessons and Activities Related to Goal:

Grade Level	Lesson Topic	Lesson Will Be Presented In Which Class/ Subject	ASCA Domain, Standard and Competency	Curriculum and Materials	Projected Start/End	Process Data (Projected number of students affected)	Perception Data (Type of surveys/ assessments to be used)	Outcome Data (Achievement, attendance and/or behavior data to be collected)	Contact Person

SMALL-GROUP ACTION PLAN

_____ Year:_____
(School Name)

Group Name: _____

Goal: _____

Target Group: _____

Data Used to Identify Students: _____

School Counselor(s)	ASCA Domain, Standard and Student Competency	Outline of Group Sessions to be Delivered	Resources Needed	Process Data (Projected number of students affected)	Perception Data (Type of surveys to be used)	Outcome Data (Achievement, attendance and/or behavior data to be collected)	Project Start/ Project End

CLOSING-THE-GAP ACTION PLAN

_____ Year:_____
(School Name)

Goal: _____

Target Group: _____

Data Used to Identify Students: _____

School Counselor(s)	ASCA Domain, Standard and Student Competency	Type of Activities to be Delivered in What Manner?	Resources Needed	Process Data (Projected number of students affected)	Perception Data (Type of surveys to be used)	Outcome Data (Achievement, attendance and/or behavior data to be collected)	Project Start/ Project End

LESSON PLAN TEMPLATE

School Counselor: _____ Date: _____

Activity: _____

Grade(s): _____

ASCA Student Standards (Domain/Standard/Competencies):

_____

_____

_____

Learning Objective(s):

1. _____

2. _____

3. _____

Materials: _____

_____

_____

Procedure:_____

_____

_____

_____

Plan for Evaluation: How will each of the following be collected?

Process Data: _____

_____

_____

Perception Data: _____

_____

_____

Outcome Data: _____

_____

_____

Follow Up: _____

_____

_____

ADDRESSING RTI VIA ASCA NATIONAL MODEL IMPLEMENTATION

By Russell A. Sabella, Ph.D., Professor, Florida Gulf Coast University

Response to intervention (RTI) is an effective, efficient, data-driven and highly collaborative process that takes advantage of the collective expertise and experiences of the school counselor, parent, RTI team and the student. Once you get to know the RTI process, you will realize it is highly consistent with all the components of comprehensive school counseling programs as espoused by the ASCA National Model. In fact, if you have been conducting closing-the-achievement-gap activities as part of your school counseling program, you are already engaged in the RTI process. You can even recognize various ASCA National Model components (e.g., data-driven decision making, multi-level prevention system, continuum of interventions, improved student outcomes, collaboration/teaming, progress monitoring and advocacy) throughout the RTI literature and within the definition of RTI.

Essentially, RTI represents a theoretical approach to identifying students who are struggling in reading, mathematics or in their behavior through action research. During the RTI process, appropriate interventions are provided and continually assessed to determine whether or not they are working and what should be done to best support and affect the student. In terms of practicality, RTI involves the participation of various school personnel including administrators, teachers, school counselors, specialists, as well as parents, who comprise the RTI team.

The RTI team identifies each struggling student's needs, develops a plan to address those needs, determines the appropriate tier (or level of intervention) necessary and meets to review data and plan the next course of action for the student. RTI's central purpose is to resolve academic or behavioral challenges through preventive measures so the student experiences success and is able to achieve developmental and grade-level goals.

The RTI process is not another initiative that will add on to the already high expectations of school counselors and all educators. RTI is not a special education pre-referral system or duty that will require all-day data crunching. And, although education has certainly witnessed some fads that have come and gone, RTI is not going away anytime soon.

ASCA has published a position statement about RTI, which highlights how school counselors recognize and consider how a student responds to intervention as part of a comprehensive school counseling program:

The Professional School Counselor and Response to Intervention (2008)

Professional school counselors implement a data-driven comprehensive school counseling program that meets the needs of all students and includes the identification of students who are at-risk for not meeting academic and behavioral expectations.

Professional school counselors design and implement plans to address the needs of struggling students and collect results data based on the effectiveness of the interventions.

Professional school counselors assist in the academic and behavioral development of students through the implementation of a comprehensive developmental school counseling program based on the ASCA National Model by:

- *Providing all students with a standards-based guidance curriculum to address universal academic, career and personal/social development*
- *Analyzing academic and behavioral data to identify struggling students*
- *Identifying and collaborating on research-based intervention strategies that are implemented by school staff*
- *Evaluating academic and behavioral progress after interventions*
- *Revising interventions as appropriate*
- *Referring to school and community services as appropriate*
- *Collaborating with administrators about RTI design and implementation*
- *Advocating for equitable education for all students and working to remove systemic barriers*

In short, RTI is an effective, efficient, data-driven and highly collaborative process that takes advantage of the collective expertise and experiences of the school counselor, parent, RTI team and the student. RTI can help school counselors garner support and promote buy-in from other stakeholders for advancing a comprehensive school counseling program.

IMPLEMENTING THE ASCA NATIONAL MODEL AT THE ELEMENTARY SCHOOL LEVEL

By Anthony Pearson, School Counselor, Sky View Elementary School, Mableton, Ga.

Elementary school counselors have a varied and dynamic role in their schools when implementing the ASCA National Model. As their time is split between classroom lessons, large-group activities, small groups and individual counseling, school counselors have the opportunity to be change agents on multiple levels through multiple delivery methods. These interactions are, of course, in addition to consultation with teachers and community, collaboration with fellow school counselors and partnerships with administration. Elementary school counselors are truly jacks-of-all-trades.

The unique position of elementary school counselors using the ASCA National Model is predicated on the ability to find an appropriate balance within their programs. In tandem with classroom guidance, elementary school counselors will also be effective in improving students' academic success through other delivery methods. If a school counselor only holds the position of "character education guidance teacher," the program will be off balance, meaning the knowledge and skills specific to school counselors won't be used to the best of their abilities. Although teaching social skills is an essential and integral part of the position, it should not be the single method of program delivery.

So how does an elementary school counselor balance the demands of classroom lessons with small groups, individual sessions and indirect student services? The simple answer is to follow the ASCA National Model's recommended use of time (see p. 44). However, the more complete answer is to figure out which students need what kind of support.

Although most students will benefit from classroom lessons and large-group activities, others will need more help. Just as all students acquire academic information in different ways, so too will students learn the career and personal/social strategies. To be most effective, an elementary school counselor should assess what delivery method is needed to make the greatest impact. The use of data (classroom behavior reports, homework completion rates or test scores) should be a driving factor in making these decisions about program delivery. As a school counselor analyzes more quantitative data, student needs often become more apparent, and the method of delivery becomes an easier decision to make.

If all students in a class except for four are consistently turning in their homework, then developing a small-group intervention for those students may be the most effective delivery method. If one student in a classroom is constantly getting referred to the office for inappropriate behavior, the most effective help may be referring him to a Big Brother program. Should a group of fifth-grade girls show relational aggression, it may require a systemwide approach including classroom lessons, individual counseling and collaboration with parents.

By adopting the ASCA National Model, school counselors can assist students in flexible, varying levels of intervention intensity. There is no one exact rigid delivery method. Each school counseling program is meant to be developed around the school's needs. The ASCA National Model allows for fluidity, creativity and logical implementation. What works at one school may not work in the exact same fashion at the next school. Of course the delivery will be provided within the ASCA National Model framework, but it is imperative that the framework is developed based on what the data indicate are in the best interests of the students at the individual school.

Here are some tips for elementary school counselors who are new to the ASCA National Model:

- **Collaborate with administration to determine areas of weakness at your school.** Are there certain students who are consistently truant? Regular visitors to the principal's office? Consider what specific activities would be beneficial for these students.
- **Quantify what you are looking to improve.** If you are running a study skills group, keep track of what group members' test scores were like prior to intervention, during intervention and after. Did student outcomes improve as the year progressed?
- **Share your results with stakeholders.** Nothing creates more buy-in to the school counseling program than the sharing of a successful plan or intervention. The more people who get on board with comprehensive school counseling programs, the more a school counselor can do for the school.
- **Defend your time.** Make sure you have a calendar that is available for others to see. The statement, "Let me look at my schedule" sends the message that the school counselor is not just in the building to put out emotional fires.
- **Always ask questions, both of your program and your school.** Where is the need? How can I deliver this in the most effective and efficient method? Who are the stakeholders with whom I need to communicate?

Elementary school counselors work hard to use all of their training and skills to create the greatest results for student success. The ASCA National Model is a road map that opens the door for any elementary school counselor who wants that kind of program.

IMPLEMENTING THE ASCA NATIONAL MODEL AT THE MIDDLE SCHOOL LEVEL

By Michelle James, School Counselor, General Smallwood Middle School, Indian Head, Md.

Too often the role of a middle school counselor is reactive and undefined. Due to this, middle school counselors are sometimes seen as a scheduler, tear wiper or lunchroom monitor. The ASCA National Model gives middle school counselors a framework they can use to guide their thinking and processes, as well as a tool to share with administrators why we do what we do. It is the foundation on which to build a middle school program.

The ASCA National Model aligns with practices in other arenas of education. When speaking with administrators and school board officials, who often do not understand the role of a school counselor, the ASCA National Model is a simple way to inform the various stakeholders how school counselors make a difference in the lives of every student. Students, data and results are at the forefront of what we do. We are no longer seen as an extra member of the school environment who can be cut in tough economic times but rather a vital member of the middle school team who helps ensure the success of all students.

Your school data are the guiding force of what is needed and how you are going to move your school forward. Through a review of my school's data, I found a focus on attendance was needed. Middle school students start to be trusted with getting up for school and getting to the bus on time without as much adult guidance. With this new-found freedom, some of my students started to take matters into their own hands, deciding they were not going to come to school as often as their parents and school staff expected. After looking at the school's data, I knew what I needed to do. Through the annual agreement and calendars, I was able to let teachers, administrators and parents know how I was addressing the issue.

Another universal topic in middle schools is bullying. Research shows doing one assembly is not an effective way of addressing bullying. Through the use of data, calendar planning, action plans and my advisory council, I was able to plan meaningful classroom lessons and small groups throughout the school year addressing this issue.

The thing I love about the ASCA National Model is that it is not cookie cutter. It doesn't tell you to do this, at this time, for these people. It is understood that each school is different, and student needs will be as varied as the schools. I cannot stress enough that you should analyze your data; the tools in the ASCA National Model will help you accomplish your goals. If all you do is what is done at another school, you have missed the mark. A program is only as good as how it is implemented.

Collaboration is key to success as a middle school counselor, particularly with administrators. Meeting with administrators weekly can be helpful in several ways. First, it helps ensure school counselors spend more time in their appropriate role. When administrators understand what you are doing and how the school counseling program will help them fulfill their role, they are more likely to let you do what you were trained to do. Second, school counselors are able to provide leadership by bringing a new perspective to problems or issues facing the school. School counselors can share strategies to help administrators "build their tool belt" to work with a student in ways that may defuse a situation rather than allowing it to become explosive. And, finally, school counselors can stay aware of policies/procedures being developed and bring leadership and advocacy for student issues into the process early on.

It is most important to collaborate with parents, which helps middle school counselors work smarter, not harder. The middle school years can be both difficult and fun times in a child's life, but the adults in their lives may not understand them or know how to work with them. A partnership with parents can help demystify these critical years and create allies on your program.

Here are some tips for implementing the ASCA National Model.
- **Tip 1:** If you have not started implementation, start. It may seem overwhelming at first, but much like riding a bike, you will get the hang of it, and it will become second nature.
- **Tip 2:** Start with one thing, such as tracking how you spend your time. This will help you gain perspective about what you do most and what needs more emphasis during the year.
- **Tip 3:** Go slowly. If you try to do everything at once, you may become overwhelmed and stop short of your goal. Remember slow and steady wins the race.
- **Tip 4:** Form your advisory council with people who are familiar with your program and will be open and honest. Consider teachers at all grade levels, in different departments and with varying years of experience. Include parents with children in different grade levels and different levels of involvement. Always include an administrator, and consider inviting the central office supervisor or a member of the board of education. Consider selecting a student from each grade level with involvement in different activities. Not only can the council help improve your program, it can also be a lot of fun and can build relationships that can prove advantageous for student support in the future.
- **Tip 5:** Get involved with your state and national association. ASCA and your state organization have a wealth of resources that will help you become a more effective school counselor via the ASCA National Model. Get involved at your level of comfort – become a member, attend conferences, join the board. After that, push yourself and go to the next level of involvement. Someone is going to be looking for your expertise and advice.
- **Tip 6:** Put your students first. Use the ASCA National Model with your school's data, and celebrate the successes.

IMPLEMENTING THE ASCA NATIONAL MODEL AT THE HIGH SCHOOL LEVEL

By Vanessa Gomez-Lee, School Counselor, Valley View High School, Moreno Valley, Calif.

According to the National Center for Education Statistics (NCES), the national average student-to-school-counselor ratio is 459-to-1. Whether your ratio is high or low, the demands of a school counselor are always high. The ASCA National Model provides a framework to meet those demands – the academic, career and personal/social needs of all students.

The beauty of the ASCA National Model is that it provides the framework for school counselors to be strategic in how they implement and create their school counseling programs. High school counselors cannot afford to do random acts of school counseling. Implementing a comprehensive program is essential for school counselors, particularly as decisions are being made regarding balancing districts' budgets. The data portion of the ASCA National Model is a great tool to show the value of having a school counselor.

At any typical high school, you will find the school counseling office is the hub and heart of a school. Effective high school counselors have to be like a superhero. At all costs school counselors advocate and support all students, which is a huge responsibility that cannot be taken lightly. Spiderman once said, "With great power comes great responsibility." The ASCA National Model provides a road map to help a high school counselor be that superhero.

One way the ASCA National Model helps high school counselors meet the needs of all students in the academic domain is through the use of data. Examining data and assessing the needs of a high school provide valuable information to help school counselors make decisions that will ensure they are meeting the needs of all students. For example, when a high school counselor looks at course placement statistics in rigorous courses, the data can help the school counselor determine the gatekeepers preventing students from becoming college and career ready. The school counselor can then develop a plan to advocate to remove those barriers and collaborate with those who have decision-making abilities related to those barriers.

The closing-the-gap action plan is another helpful tool for high school counselors. By utilizing this template, a high school counselor can create a data-driven plan that addresses the issues high school counselors frequently face, such as dropout prevention. For example, school counselors can develop a closing-the-gap action plan to address the needs of incoming freshmen who struggled in middle school, listing the goals and competencies to achieve, activities delivered, resources needed and method of evaluation. The plan requires collaboration with middle school counselors. Working together helps ensure an easier transition from middle to high school and leads to better results for students.

The results report template can help high school counselors determine the success of their interventions. After reviewing process, perception and outcome data, the high school counselor can determine the level of success of the activities in the plan and consider the implications for the future. This data can be shared with all stakeholders, which can create a win-win situation. The results data can show that students are getting the help they need while increasing the awareness of stakeholders of the important work school counselors do.

Benefits of using the ASCA National Model at the high school level include:

- **Limiting non-school-counseling duties.** Assigning extensive non-school-counseling activities to high school counselors can affect their ability to meet the needs of all students. After conducting the use-of-time assessment, high school counselors can share that data with their administrators and have an honest discussion about the role of a school counselor and the program goals.

- **Getting administrator support.** Administrator support is essential when implementing the ASCA National Model, and involving your administrator in the process is crucial. The ASCA National Model has several components that promote administrator involvement and understanding. The foundation component encourages the school counseling team to link school counseling program mission, vision and goals with the school's and district's mission, vision and goals. The annual agreement is an extremely effective tool to ensure school counselors and administrators are on the same page with program development, organization and goals. Conducting the yearly program assessment not only helps school counselors evaluate where they are with implementation of the ASCA National Model, but it also can be used to provide administrators a clearer picture of the work school counselors do.

- **Using data in your advocacy efforts.** Evaluating existing data such as test scores, attendance rate, suspension rates, etc. provides school counselors with information needed to become agents of change. Often school communities do not want to admit that not all students are successful or that their school has safety or drug issues. High school counselors can use data as a catalyst to improving achievement and the school climate. Data help school counselors advocate for their students as well as for their profession. High school counselors can garner support from their school board by presenting their results data and showing how the work they do connects to the district's mission and goals.

- **Staying organized.** Organization is crucial to a successful school counseling program. To meet the needs of all high school students, school counselors deliver services in a variety of ways, including classroom presentations, small-group activities and individual counseling. Managing and maintaining weekly and annual calendars is crucial to successfully delivering these services. How high school counselors manage their time has a significant impact on whether or not program goals are met.

- **Improving teamwork.** Any team of high school counselors will have strengths and weaknesses. The ASCA National Model supports high school counselors working together as a team, building on each school counselor's strengths and supporting each other's weaknesses. Collaboration on ASCA National Model components is a great way to develop stronger goals and plans and get better results. Connecting with other district initiatives such as professional learning communities is an excellent way to implement components of the ASCA National Model.

Delivery System

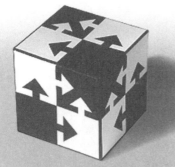

Topics Include:

Direct Student Services
- School Counseling Core Curriculum
- Individual Student Planning
- Responsive Services

Indirect Student Services
- Referrals
- Consultation
- Collaboration

The delivery component focuses on the method of implementing the school counseling program to students. This section describes the services and strategies school counselors provide to students and interactions they have with others as they work to promote student achievement, equity and access for all students.

The delivery component consists of direct and indirect student services. Direct services are provided with students, and indirect services are provided for students.

- **Direct student services** are in-person interactions between school counselors and students. Through the direct services components of school counseling core curriculum, individual student planning and responsive services, school counselors help students develop the knowledge, attitudes and skills identified from the school counseling core curriculum.

- **Indirect student services** are services provided on behalf of students as a result of the school counselor's interactions with others. Through indirect services, school counselors provide leadership, advocacy and collaboration, which enhance student achievement and promote systemic change related to equity and access.

It is recommended that 80 percent or more of the school counselor's time be spent in direct and indirect student services. See the Use of Time section in the Management component for more detailed information.

Figure 4.1 Delivery Component

Item	Elements and Strategies	Recipient	Method
Direct Student Services	School Counseling Core Curriculum ■ Instruction ■ Group Activities Individual Student Planning ■ Appraisal ■ Advisement Responsive Services ■ Counseling ■ Crisis Response	All Students DATA DRIVEN Identified Students	Interactions with Students in: Large Group Classroom Small Group Individual
Indirect Student Services	■ Referrals ■ Consultation ■ Collaboration	All Students DATA DRIVEN Identified Students	Interactions with Others

Adapted from Gysbers, N.C. & Henderson, P. (2012) Developing and managing your school counseling program (5th ed.), Alexandria, VA: American Counseling Association.

DIRECT STUDENT SERVICES

Direct student services are delivered through three elements: school counseling core curriculum, individual student planning and responsive services (Gysbers & Henderson, 2012). School counselors review school data to inform decisions about strategies to use within each element based on students' needs.

Direct student services of the school counseling program include activities that promote academic, career and personal/social development. These activities are provided to all students in the school. In addition, school counselors use data to identify students with achievement, attendance or behavioral needs impeding student success. Additional program activities and services are provided to these students to address their specific needs.

School counselors also use data to determine how the school counseling activities will be delivered. To reach the whole student body or entire grade levels, school counselors focus on classroom or large-group settings. For more student-specific activities, school counselors focus on small group or individual settings.

School Counseling Core Curriculum

The school counseling core curriculum consists of a planned, written instructional program that is comprehensive in scope, preventive in nature and developmental in design. School counselors plan, design and evaluate the curriculum. The curriculum is delivered to every student by school counselors and other educators as appropriate.

The school counseling core curriculum facilitates the systematic delivery of lessons or activities aligned with the school counseling program's vision, mission and goals. The curriculum promotes knowledge, attitudes and skills of student competencies appropriate to student developmental levels through instruction in three content areas: academic achievement, career development and personal/social growth.

The school counseling core curriculum is established through design, implementation and documentation. See the School Counseling Action Plan section in the Management component for more information on design and documentation.

The school counseling core curriculum is delivered through such strategies as:

- **Instruction:** School counselors provide direct instruction, team teach or assist in teaching the school counseling core curriculum, learning activities or units in classrooms or other school facilities. They may also provide follow-up to small groups or individual students as needed.

- **Group activities:** School counselors conduct planned activities outside the classroom to promote academic, career or personal/social development, such as college and career fairs, post-secondary site visits, student team building/leadership workshops, community/business tours.

Individual Student Planning

Individual student planning consists of ongoing systemic activities designed to help students establish personal goals and develop future plans, such as individual learning plans and graduation plans. School counselors use these activities to help all students plan, monitor and manage their own learning as well as to achieve academic, career and personal/social competencies aligned with the school counseling core curriculum.

Through individual student planning, school counselors assist students as the students evaluate educational, career and personal goals. School counselors promote individual student planning by helping students develop individual learning plans, make the transition from elementary to middle, middle to high or make the transition from school to higher education or work. Activities may be delivered on an individual basis, in small groups or classroom settings. Parents or guardians and other school personnel are often included in the activities.

Individual student planning is implemented through such strategies as:

- **Appraisal** – School counselors work with students to analyze and evaluate their abilities, interests, skills and achievement. Test information and other data are often used as the basis for helping students develop immediate and long-range plans.

- **Advisement** – School counselors help students make decisions for future plans based on academic, career and personal/social data.

Responsive Services

Responsive services consist of activities designed to meet students' immediate needs and concerns. This component is available to all students and may be initiated by students, teachers or parents or by school counselors after a review of data.

Responsive services are designed to help students resolve academic, career and personal/social issues and are delivered through such strategies as:

- **Counseling** – School counselors provide counseling sessions in individual or small-group settings to help students overcome issues impeding achievement or success. The counseling process helps students identify problems, causes, alternatives and possible consequences so they can make decisions and take appropriate actions.

  Counseling is planned and goal-focused, and it is short-term in nature. School counselors do not provide therapy or long-term counseling in schools to address psychological disorders. Therapy, or therapeutic treatment, is defined as "remedial treatment of mental or bodily disorder" (Merriam-Webster, 2012).

  However, school counselors are prepared to recognize and respond to student mental health crises and needs and to address these barriers to student success by offering education, prevention and crisis and short-term intervention until the student is connected with available community resources. When students require long-term counseling or therapy, school counselors make referrals to appropriate community resources (ASCA, 2009).

- **Crisis Response** – School counselors provide support and assistance to students as they navigate critical and emergency situations. Crisis response includes intervention and follow-up to the immediate needs and is designed to prevent the situation from becoming more severe. There are often written procedures provided by the school or district that are to be used in crisis situations.

INDIRECT STUDENT SERVICES

School counselors provide indirect student services as a means to support student achievement and to promote equity and access for all students. While students are the beneficiaries of indirect services, school counselors work with a variety of people to deliver these services. School counselors may interact with parents, teachers, administrators, school staff and community stakeholders in order to promote student achievement for a specific student or to promote systemic change to address the needs of underachieving or underrepresented groups of students in the school.

Through indirect student services, school counselors gather or share information about student developmental issues, problems and successes. When a situation requires a school counselor to share information that could identify a specific student, school counselors receive student or parent permission or take significant precautions to protect student confidentiality following ASCA's Ethical Standards for School Counselors (ASCA, 2010).

Indirect student services are delivered through such strategies as:

- **Referrals** – School counselors direct students and parents to school or community resources for additional assistance or information through referrals. School referral sources may include academic support such as tutoring; career support such as college planning Web sites or employment training; and personal/social support such as community agencies that treat mental health issues including suicidal ideation, violence, abuse and depression.

- **Consultation** – School counselors share strategies that support student achievement with parents, teachers, other educators and community organizations through consultation. School counselors also serve as student advocates to promote academic, career and personal/social development through this strategy. Finally, school counselors use consultation to receive information on student needs and to identify strategies that promote student achievement.

- **Collaboration** – School counselors work with other educators, parents and the community to support student achievement and advocate for equity and access for all students through collaboration. School counselors may collaborate in a variety of ways including:

  - *Teaming and partnering:* School counselors work with staff, parents, businesses and community organizations to support student achievement and fulfill the goals of the school counseling program. Teaming and partnering can occur through simple resource sharing, joint presentations, advisory councils or formalized partnerships with specific focus or agenda.

  - *School/district committees:* By serving on committees or advisory boards, school counselors advocate for student programs and resources and assist in generating schoolwide and district support for the school counseling program.

- *Parent workshops:* School counselors facilitate or organize informational sessions about student developmental issues for parents or guardians to address the needs of the school community and to reflect the school counseling core curriculum.

References

American School Counselor Association (2010). *Ethical standards for school counselors.* Alexandria, VA: Author.

American School Counselor Association (2009). The professional school counselor and student mental health. *Position Statements.* Retrieved May 7, 2012 from http://www.schoolcounselor.org/content.asp?pl=325&sl=127&contentid=178.

Gysbers, N. C. & Henderson, P. (2012) *Developing and managing your school counseling program* (5th ed.), Alexandria, VA: American Counseling Association.

therapy. 2012. In Merriam-Webster.com. Retrieved May 8, 2012 from http://www.merriam-webster.com/dictionary/therapy.

PROVIDING STUDENT SERVICES

By Marrius Pettiford, Ph.D., Director of Student Support Services, Alamance-Burlington School System, Burlington, N.C.

School counselors can be effective members and leaders of student services teams through implementation of the ASCA National Model. The ASCA National Model's focus on leadership, advocacy, collaboration and systemic change sets the stage for school counselors to have a significant impact on the work of the student service team.

Student services, sometimes referred to as student support services or pupil services, include prevention, intervention, transition and follow-up services for students and families. These services are delivered by a variety of staff members, including school counselors, school social workers, school nurses, school psychologists and other staff such as drop-out prevention coordinators/counselors, career development coordinators and college access counselors/advisors.

The ASCA National Model can and has been adapted as a framework for the student services team to increase collaboration and teamwork. Each of the items in the foundation, delivery, management and accountability components are completed as a group and submitted by the group to show their collaborative efforts to promote student achievement and success. The plan, and the results of the plan, belong to the group and demonstrate how effective student services can be when delivered.

Collaboration and advocacy are the essential unifying themes that delineate the school counselors' role on the student services teams. The interdisciplinary nature of the student services team provides an excellent opportunity for school counselors to demonstrate their school leadership and collaboration. School counselors can be leaders in helping the team develop specific goals drawing on the strengths of all team members to deliver the most effective prevention and intervention strategies.

For example, after reviewing data, a school counselor may identify school attendance as a barrier to student academic success. The school counselor would engage the team in a conversation about how to best address the issue, inviting other members of the team to think of strategies they could provide based on their own professional skill set. The school social worker may conduct a home visit to determine if there are any supports the family may need to get students to school each day on time. The school nurse could determine if there are any health issues that may affect the student or family. The school psychologist may work with the school counselor in conducting a support group. The school administrator is made aware of the personal/social issue that may affect the student and family and works with teachers to ensure proper adjustments in instruction take place for the success of the student.

School counselors can utilize the framework of the ASCA National Model to provide a structure for data-driven decision making. The components of the ASCA National Model can be utilized with student services teams to identify the groups of students who may need additional interventions based on school-specific data. Even though the work may be completed by multiple staff members, the end result is that the school counselor has brought attention to and addressed a specific issue or gap through implementation of the ASCA National Model. In addition, sharing the curriculum action plan with other collaborators may garner additional supporters in implementing strategies that support student success and achievement.

Student advocacy can also be an effective role of student services teams. Using school data to highlight the reality of school policies and procedures that are barriers to access for all students is a cornerstone of student advocacy. School counselors can take a leadership role in advocating for the removal of barriers to education for all students by voicing their concerns to the team. The additional stakeholders on the team may then have an increased influence on the school community to gain support for addressing and removing barriers to opportunities and learning.

Following are some tips to gain support from other student support services staff:
- Start building a relationship with other support services staff.
- Talk with each other to determine if there are areas of service duplication.
- Talk with each other to determine if there are opportunities to collaborate.
- Use the ASCA National Model executive summary to educate staff about the ASCA National Model.
- Develop a schedule for weekly meetings to discuss how to assist your students and school community.
- Share your annual agreement with student support services staff as a template of what they could use with the principal.
- Ask other student support services staff to join you at ASCA National Model trainings.
- Discuss ways the team can present to school staff at the beginning of the year to explain each role and how you work together.

ENHANCING THE SCHOOL COUNSELOR/PRINCIPAL RELATIONSHIP WITH AN ANNUAL AGREEMENT

By Linda Brannan, K-12 Student Support Services Consultant, North Carolina Department of Public Instruction

Today's school counselors are leaders, advocates, collaborators and systemic change agents. The ASCA National Model emphasizes that school counselors should not work in isolation but instead engage in cooperative efforts with stakeholders to implement programs that meet all students' needs and support their school's mission.

Principals have considerable influence on shaping their school counselors' role. A key component to the school counselor's leadership role is a collaborative relationship with the principal. New attitudes about school counselors and principals joining forces for leadership and advocacy can have a positive impact on the mission and climate of the school in delivering academic success.

School counselors and principals are strong allies in supporting students' equitable access to a rigorous academic program. As part of the principal's educational leadership team, the school counselor's role is crucial in supporting academic achievement as school counselors are seen as proactive leaders and advocates for student success.

The College Board, the National Association of Secondary Principals and ASCA agree that the school counselor/principal relationship is a dynamic and organic relationship that evolves over time in response to a school's ever-changing needs. A 2011 toolkit developed collaboratively between the three organizations encourages school counselors and principals to use the strength of the relationship to collaboratively lead school reform efforts to increase achievement for all students. The desired outcome of an effective principal/school counselor relationship is to raise achievement levels for all students and ensure equity in educational outcomes. The toolkit promotes four critical areas for the principal and school counselor to address to effectively work together: communication, trust/respect, leadership and collaborative planning. An effective school counselor/principal relationship is characterized by a shared vision of student success, collaboration, high mutual professional regard, where the principal considers the school counselor a valued, trusted resource.

DELIVERY

Collaboration between principals and school counselors is an essential strategy toward reaching the common vision where "every student learns, achieves and is prepared to graduate with 21st-century skills, college- and career-ready." ASCA National Model implementation strengthens the relationship and supports collaboration around the common goals shared by school counselors and principals.

A key tool for collaboration in the ASCA National Model is the annual agreement. The agreement provides an opportunity for school counselors to share proposed goals and outcomes of the data-driven comprehensive school counseling program with their principals. School counselors create and present to their principal a yearly draft of their school counseling plan, indicating how they will collaborate with various stakeholders such as administrators, teachers, parents and the community. During this meeting, the school counselor and principal review and revise the goals, objectives and strategies of the data-driven school counseling plan to meet the needs of the students and the school improvement plan. The principal discusses the annual agreement with the school counselor, and they arrive at consensus regarding on topics such as:

▪ School counseling strategies to meet the needs of students and the school
▪ How students will be assigned to school counselors in the school
▪ How the comprehensive school counseling program will be delivered

This collaborative annual agreement helps principals and school counselors reach consensus on the annual goals, program delivery and means of accountability for the school counseling program.

The process of completing the annual agreement addresses the four areas of the College Board/NASSP/ASCA toolkit and provides a model for day-to-day practice. School counselors and principals may decide to include items in the agreement such as scheduled meeting times and preferred communication patterns (e-mails, phone calls, meeting agendas, etc.) with various stakeholders such as the advisory council, faculty, parents, the school leadership team and, of course, each other. These communication patterns and scheduled collaborative meetings provide ongoing opportunities for principals and school counselors to review process, perception and outcome data. In addition, these school-specific areas of collaborative planning lead to discussions about their respective roles in the school.

Although school counselors and principals may have separate and specific roles and responsibilities, there is much overlap with regard to accomplishing common goals for the school and students. When principals and school counselors meet and agree on program priorities, implementation strategies and the organization of the school counseling department, the entire program will produce the desired results for students as decisions are made based on the school site needs and data analysis.

Mutual trust and respect are developed through the conversations of role definition, collaborative planning and formulation of the annual agreement. By reviewing school data, which indicate the needs of students and the school; establishing a shared vision as to the implementation of strategies to meet these needs; and communicating this shared vision to stakeholders, the principal and school counselor collaborate and serve as leaders for improving student achievement and promoting systemic change in their school.

COLLEGE AND CAREER READINESS AND THE ASCA NATIONAL MODEL

By Don Fraser Jr., Director of Education and Training, National Association for College Admission Counseling

School counselors have the opportunity to be leaders in making education equitable for all students. College and career readiness is a key area of equity and access that is receiving increasing attention across the country. Although school counselors have often been omitted from conversations related to education reform, the steady growth and acceptance of the ASCA National Model in districts across the country, as well as an influx of new school counselors who have been trained in the framework, has created conditions where school counselors are positioned to be leaders and agents of systemic change now more than ever before. School counselors must use their skills to ensure all students are college- and career-ready, especially those who have been consistently marginalized by our educational system.

Recent research states that by 2018 the U.S. will need at least 4.7 million new workers with post-secondary certificates. Students must continue their education beyond high school and attain a degree to be competitive in tomorrow's workforce. Yet, going to college is still not a foregone conclusion for many high school students. And although many historically underrepresented populations have made significant gains in enrolling and completing college, gaps still exist between their white peers. School counselors can play a major role in closing this attainment gap.

As education shifts its attention to college and career readiness, the ASCA National Model helps school counselors provide leadership in that shift, in ways that are appropriate for school counselors. The ASCA National Model core components ensure schools have a comprehensive school counseling program with measureable goals and outcomes. In addition, the research-based approach helps to continue to promote the appropriate role of the school counselor.

Below are some notable elements from the ASCA National Model that will promote college and career readiness.

Foundation

- Writing vision and mission statements encouraging college and career readiness for all students sets the stage for all students to develop the skills necessary to be successful in higher education and the workplace. The movement toward college and career readiness for all requires schools to examine their mission, culture, curriculum and staff.
- Developing program goals through the use of data is more important than ever. If you are not using data (of all kinds) to inform your school counseling program, then achieving college and career readiness for all is unlikely. School counselors must first take a critical look at their school's data before making a determination about the content and direction of their program.
- Considering how other student standards support and enhance the school counseling program is important. School counselors often have to meet multiple sets of standards for student development and achievement simultaneously while ensuring their program is nimble enough to navigate a changing landscape.

Management

- The school data profile helps school counselors track achievement, attendance, behavior and school safety data to identify strengths and areas for improvement. Students' college and career readiness is being measured and heavily scrutinized, so a school counselor's ability to track and demonstrate data associated with college and career readiness is crucial.
- Curriculum, small-group and closing-the-gap action plans can be developed with a specific focus on supporting college and career readiness. These plans help school counselors design, document, implement and evaluate the effectiveness of college- and career-readiness initiatives.
- The school counseling program assessment and school counselor competencies assessment take center stage in moving your program forward. As incorporating effective college- and career-readiness activities into a school counseling program may be a new frontier for some, these assessments help school counselors understand areas needed for professional development to ensure they possess the core knowledge and skills needed to best support students. In addition, it is increasingly important to determine if your program is working.

Delivery

- The school counseling core curriculum and individual student planning elements and strategies are where the rubber hits the road for college and career readiness – how school counselors make it happen and bring their program to life. Although many outside of the school counseling department may judge you based upon what they see you doing, it is important to keep these key components in mind and not be seduced by the temptation to develop something that simply sounds impressive. To effectively address and develop college and career readiness, school counselors must do their work up front, designing an appropriate curriculum and including effective individual student planning activities that ensure appropriate results are achieved.

Accountability

- The school data profile analysis informs school counseling goals and helps school counselors identify any areas where systemic changes may be needed. Tracking data is a recurring theme across the ASCA National Model, and the tips offered here are helpful to school counselors looking to improve their programs.
- Use-of-time analysis informs school counseling program decisions about how to best meet and anticipate the needs of all students in the future.
- Curriculum, small-group and closing-the-gap results reports help school counselors show how students are different as a result of their program and demonstrate school counselors are central figures in schools – educators who have a positive impact on the educational outcomes of their students. These results reports can play a major role in showing the impact of the school counseling program on college and career readiness.

Education is at a critical crossroad, and it must evolve as it has during other such junctures in our history (e.g., the Industrial Revolution and the Race to Space). What lies before school counselors is the opportunity to be leaders in making education equitable for those who have been consistently marginalized by our educational system. As our country becomes increasingly diverse, we have an obligation to get it right, so all students can be college- and career-ready. And although we have made significant strides recently toward this goal, to reach it, all educators, particularly school counselors, must examine and identify their role so they are a part of the movement rather than a casualty of it.

STEM EDUCATION AND THE ASCA NATIONAL MODEL

By Mark Boggie, Assistant Dean of Student Services, Cochise Community College, Sierra Vista, Ariz.

Since the early 1980s, the United States has attempted to address the declining performance of students in assessments of science, technology, engineering and mathematics (STEM) area content knowledge. Compared with students in countries we had traditionally outperformed, our students are lagging. America now finds itself in 24th place in science assessments and 28th in mathematics assessments. America is also falling behind in the number of science and engineering degrees awarded to its students. As a result, STEM education has been at the forefront of political initiatives and reforms occurring in the American education community.

School counselors implementing a comprehensive school counseling program can serve in a grassroots effort to ignite student interest in STEM career fields. The goals of STEM education – to encourage more students to have an interest in science-related fields and to complete degrees in those fields – can easily be incorporated into the program goals of the foundation of a school counseling program. In doing so, school counselors can systemically encourage students with interests and abilities in STEM areas to continue those pursuits.

School counselors can also encourage students to consider STEM-related fields through the management component of the ASCA National Model. When developing curriculum action plans, school counselors can focus on competencies from the ASCA Student Standards that might lead to career exploration of STEM-related fields. The standards, addressing academic, career and personal/social domains, form the basis of the plan school counselors use to organize stand-alone lessons related to STEM topics or, more preferably, in conjunction with lesson plans already taught by STEM classroom teachers. This type of collaboration can have a profound effect on the choices students make.

ASCA's partner in STEM education, the Sally Ride Science Foundation, has developed a framework for assisting school counselors in this process, collaborating with classroom teachers of science, mathematics and technology. Using simple, easy-to-understand methods of infusing STEM education into the current curriculum, school counselors can help students discover the wide range of careers in STEM fields. The research-based Sally Ride Science Academy Framework provides four basic strategies to introduce STEM careers and the scientists involved in them in a way that aligns with the teaching and learning process.

Step One: Guide students in exploring the wide variety of science careers – Students need information about the many types of careers in the STEM areas. As STEM lessons are introduced, classroom teachers and school counselors can develop resources presenting the wide array of STEM careers. Some careers combine interests and science, like photography and biology, and some are cross-discipline, like oceanography or bioengineering. Students can also take many paths that lead to a STEM career ranging from one-year technical training to a doctoral or professional degree. Recent research has shown that schools implementing a comprehensive school counseling program with a career development focus for student/parent decision making produce a variety of positive outcomes including improved attendance and increased adademic success.

Step Two: Introduce students to diverse scientists – Help students imagine themselves as scientists and engineers. It's important for students to understand that people working in science today are regular people just like them, coming from all walks of life and taking many different paths to their science careers. It is helpful when school counselors break the stereotypes of scientists that many students believe, such as scientists working alone in a lab and doing nothing but research. Students may find the reality to be far more interesting. Many scientists work in collaborative environments or out in the field, outside any lab room. STEM careers depend on teamwork, creativity and flexibility, characteristics students don't always associate with STEM. It is also helpful if students can relate to role models in STEM careers who are like them.

Step Three: Help students get to know themselves better – School counselors can play an integral role in developing students' self-image. Through individual student planning, school counselors can help students understand their strengths and interests, as well as their preferences in work environment. School counselors encourage students to explore who they are, find their interests, look for careers that match their interests and help plan their short- and long-term goals.

Step Four: Help students map out their goals – Also through individual student planning school counselors help students make decisions about their future that have long-lasting impact. Many states have mandated that students develop an educational plan mapping out their course path, post-secondary plan and possible career path. School counselors can have an impact on issues of systemic change, closing achievement, opportunity and attainment gaps, by being active participants in these plans and helping students choose coursework in middle and high school that will lead to college and career readiness for STEM-related careers. School counselors can also support achievement in these courses by promoting academic success skills and providing referrals if students need extra help. Schools and school districts may set goals to improve academic achievement in STEM-related areas, and school counselors can collaborate with the school community in reaching those goals. Goals such as increasing the number of students who pursue a major in STEM careers could lead the school counselor to collect or review data on the majors selected by recent graduates. These data could become helpful baseline data to compare after implementing programs or activities designed to highlight STEM careers and could be a component of the school data profile in the accountability component.

School counselors can help students be prepared for the future by collaborating with STEM teachers and providing needed information for students to make informed choices. This collaboration naturally includes guiding students in exploring the wide variety of science careers, introducing students to diverse scientists, helping students get to know themselves better and assisting students in mapping out their goals.

Accountability

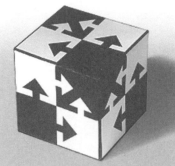

Topics Include:

Data Analysis
- School Data Profile Analysis
- Use-of-Time Analysis

Program Results
- Curriculum Results Analysis
- Small-Group Results Analysis
- Closing-the-Gap Results Analysis

Evaluation and Improvement
- School Counselor Competencies Assessment Analysis
- Program Assessment Analysis
- School Counselor Performance Appraisal

To achieve the best results for students, school counselors regularly evaluate their program to determine its effectiveness. School counselors use this evaluation to answer the question, "How are students different as a result of the school counseling program?" Now more than ever, school counselors are expected to demonstrate the effectiveness of their programs in measurable terms.

School counselors implement data-driven comprehensive school counseling programs using accountability strategies to monitor student achievement, to continually evaluate and improve their school counseling program and to demonstrate the impact their program is having on students (Dimmit, Carey, & Hatch, 2007; Dimmit 2009; Holcomb-McCoy, 2007; House & Hayes, 2002; Rowell, 2006; Ward, 2009; Ware & Galassi, 2006; Young & Kaffenberger, 2011). Accountability skills also help school counselors "garner the political clout necessary to improve school-counselor-to-student staffing ratios and redefine school counselor roles and activities..." (Hatch & Chen-Hayes, 2008, p. 39; Dimmit et al., 2007).

The purpose of this component is to analyze the data that have been collected and make program decisions based on the analysis. There are three sections:
- Data Analysis
- Program Results
- Evaluation and Improvement

DATA ANALYSIS

Data analysis informs decisions about the school counseling program. Data are reviewed over time to inform the school counselor about student needs and school and community trends. The school data profile and the use-of-time assessment are reviewed annually to evaluate and improve the school counseling program, and they can be an effective part of end-of-year program evaluation and goal setting for the following school year.

School Data Profile Analysis

The school data profile is a summary of the school's achievement, attendance, behavior and safety record over a multiyear period and can contribute to a better understanding of trends at the school. Analysis of the school data profile helps school counselors monitor student achievement, identify achievement, opportunity and attainment gaps and recognize a need for systemic change (Holcomb-McCoy, 2007; Rowell, 2006). School data profile analysis can also be used to inform school counseling program goals.

Consider the following questions when analyzing your data:
- What strengths are indicated by the data at your school?
- What concerns are raised about the data?
- Do achievement gaps exist?
- Have attendance rates changed?
- What can you learn from examining the safety data?
- How is your school counseling program addressing the gaps?
- How can the school counseling program contribute to closing the gaps or addressing the educational issues posed by the data?
- What additional data are needed to fully understand an educational issue and identify a school counseling intervention? (VSCA, 2008)

The first school data profile that is completed becomes the baseline from which to measure future school counseling program results. Yearly updates assess both program progress and impact. The information reveals school counseling program strengths and weaknesses as well as growth or loss in overall student success. The school data profile is also a convenient tool for sharing systemic change, programmatic successes and student needs.

Analyzing the school data profile is valuable for all school counselors in the building. All school counselors need to understand how the data were collected and how to interpret the data, implications of the data and their role in the plan to address the data.

Consider the example of a middle school data profile and what we can learn about the school's strengths and weaknesses by examining the data over a three-year period (see Middle School Data Profile p. 109).

Use-of-time Assessment Analysis

Analysis of the use-of-time assessment informs many components of a comprehensive school counseling program such as the annual agreement; calendars; and curriculum, small-group and closing-the-gap action plans. It is recommended that school counselors spend 80 percent or more of their time in direct and indirect student services, such as school counseling core curriculum, individual student planning, responsive services, referrals, consultation and collaboration, and 20 percent or less of their time in program management tasks such as committee work, calendaring, data collection/analysis, planning and fair-share responsibilities. Completing the use-of-time assessment twice a year will help school counselors determine how their time is spent.

The analysis of the use-of-time assessment may inform many program decisions, but it is especially useful when considering the following:

1. How close am I to allocating at least 80 percent of my time to serving students?
2. Is the amount of time allocated to any particular service delivery the most effective use of my time?
3. Are the selected delivery methods and strategies the best use of school counselor time that will lead to the accomplishment of identified goals?

While spending 80 percent of time in direct and indirect student services is the general recommendation for a balanced school counseling program, use of time within the 80 percent may look different from school to school based on school data. Decisions about how to allocate school counseling program time are based on student needs as demonstrated in the school data profile and alignment with school and school counseling program goals.

> For example, after analyzing the school data profile, a school counselor in a high-needs school may determine it would be more effective to spend a higher percentage of time than recommended on strategies from indirect student services to best meet the needs of all students in the school.

It is suggested that for two weeks each year, such as one week in the fall and one in the spring, school counselors estimate the number of hours they are engaged in direct and indirect student services during those weeks to determine how close they are to the ideal of 80 percent. After determining the approximate percentage of time, school counselors can reflect on the effectiveness of program delivery methods and strategies and adjust as needed. The analysis can also be used to promote a discussion about the most effective use of school counselor time with administrators. It can also be a helpful tool when completing a school counseling program evaluation, which informs program improvement.

In summary, data analysis informs the comprehensive school counseling program. Analyzing the school data profile and use-of-time assessment are strategies that can be used at any stage of program implementation or evaluation. They are also an effective part of end-of-year program evaluation and goal setting for the following school year.

PROGRAM RESULTS

Analyzing school counseling program results reports ensures programs are evaluated for effectiveness and informs decisions related to program improvement. The analysis of results reports is the heart of having a data-driven school counseling program. Analyzing the data from results reports will contribute to more focused programming, more effective interventions and a more responsive school counseling program.

Three types of results reports are created based on action plans developed as part of program management activities:

1. Curriculum Results Report
2. Small-Group Results Report
3. Closing-the-Gap Results Report

Data collection provides the school counseling program with the information needed to evaluate the program as it relates to student progress. Data analysis helps school counselors determine what worked and what didn't and clarifies what needs to be changed or improved.

Action plan data are collected throughout the implementation of the plan. Three types of data are reported: process, perception and outcome data. The purpose of data analysis is to determine the extent of change in student learning and behavior and to use the data to promote systemic change as needed. School counselors demonstrate their leadership and advocacy roles as they use the findings from results reports to reduce or remove barriers to learning.

Type of Data	Definition	Examples
Process	■ Number of participants involved ■ Number of times the intervention took place ■ Evidence that an event occurred	30 students participated in six classroom lessons
Perception	■ Asks what participants think they know, believe or can do ■ Collected through surveys that measure self-reports of attainment of competencies, attitudes and beliefs and perceived gains in knowledge	■ Pre-post tests ■ Needs assessments ■ Program evaluation surveys ■ Feedback surveys *Example* – 59 percent of fifth-graders feel safe at school
Outcome	■ Shows the impact of an intervention ■ Reports the extent to which the program has had a positive impact on students' ability to utilize their knowledge, attitudes and skills to effect improvement in achievement, attendance and behavior ■ Collected from multiple sources	■ Promotion rates ■ Attendance rates ■ Number of discipline referrals ■ Grade-point averages ■ Student graduation rates *Example* – 79 percent of the senior class was accepted into a four-year college

See Program Results Data section of the Management component for a more detailed description of process, perception and outcome data.

Results report data analysis follows the completion of an action plan and helps school counselors evaluate the impact of the action plan. School counselors typically review results reports in the spring of each school year at a minimum and use them to inform goal setting for the following year.

Analysis of the Curriculum Results Report

Analysis of the curriculum results report demonstrates the effectiveness of program and classroom activities and informs program improvement.

The curriculum results report serves as a tool for:
- Ensuring the program was carried out as planned
- Ensuring every student was served
- Ensuring developmentally appropriate materials were used
- Documenting the program's process, perception and outcome data
- Analyzing the activities' effectiveness
- Sharing the impact of the curriculum
- Improving activity or program
- Advocating for systemic change

The following questions may be helpful when analyzing curriculum results reports:
- Were appropriate learning goals identified? Did the choice of curriculum and/or activities support the goals?
- What can be learned from analyzing the process data? (e.g., Did all students receive the curriculum? Were the scheduled sessions conducted?)
- What can be learned from analyzing the perception data? (e.g., Did the curriculum meet the goals of teaching knowledge, attitudes and skills? Did students report an increase in knowledge of lesson content? Do pre- and post-test results indicate there was an increase in learning?)
- What can be learned from analyzing the outcome data? (e.g., What impact did the curriculum have on achievement, attendance or behavioral data, such as GPA, report card data, state testing, discipline referrals, safety report and attendance?)
- After reviewing the results report, what are the implications or recommendations?

Analysis of the Small-Group Results Report

Small-group counseling is an effective intervention school counselors can implement to address specific student academic and behavioral needs (Whiston & Quinby, 2009). Analysis of the small-group results report helps school counselors report the impact and effectiveness of the small-group intervention.

The following questions may be helpful when analyzing small-group results reports:
- Were the right goals identified for the group of students? Did the choice of activities and/or interventions support the goals?
- What can be learned from analyzing the process data? (e.g., Did the size of the group, the amount of time or the number of sessions affect the outcome data? What changes might need to be made should this intervention be used again?)

- What can be learned from analyzing the perception data? (e.g., Did the curriculum meet the goals? Did students report an increase in knowledge of lesson content? Do pre- and post-test outcome data indicate there was an increase in learning?)
- What can be learned from analyzing the outcome data? (e.g., What impact did the curriculum have on achievement, attendance or behavioral data?)
- Reviewing the results report, what are the implications or recommendations?

Analysis of the Closing-the-Gap Results Report

Closing-the-gap activities address important issues of equity and student achievement. Therefore one of the most important aspects of program analysis rests with analyzing the closing-the-gap results. Closing-the-gap results report analysis helps school counselors report the impact and effectiveness of program activities and inform program improvement.

The following questions may be helpful when analyzing closing-the-gap results reports:
- What can be learned from analyzing the process data? (e.g., Did all students receive the intervention? Were the scheduled sessions conducted? How many students had access to rigorous course work? Did this number increase?)
- What can be learned from analyzing the perception data? (e.g. Did the curriculum meet the goals? Did students report an increase in knowledge of lesson content? Do pre- and post-test outcome data indicate there was an increase in learning?)
- What can be learned from analyzing the outcome data? (e.g., What impact did the intervention have on achievement, attendance or behavioral data?)
- Reviewing the results report, what are the implications or recommendations?

Collecting data and analyzing results are key strategies to assess program effectiveness. School counselors must be able to determine student progress toward data-driven goals to continue to support student achievement. Results reports can be powerful advocacy tools when promoting the school counseling program.

Sharing Results

After data have been collected and analyzed, it is important to consider how to use the data and how to share it with others. Results reports can take on many forms and be disseminated in several ways such as:
- Web sites
- One-page handouts
- Part of a larger report to administrators and school board members
- Presentation to faculty
- Part of the school's or district's data materials

Regularly sharing results reports about the impact of the school counseling program with administrators, faculty and the school community in a document or in five- to 10-minute presentations will likely promote understanding, increase the value of and promote respect and indispensability for the work of professional school counselors (Dimmit, Carey & Hatch, 2007; Young & Kaffenberger, 2009).

When sharing results, it is important to remember that changes in student knowledge, attitudes, skills or behavior may be the result of numerous factors. School counselors are encouraged to communicate the ways they are contributing in a meaningful way to the overall academic achievement of students. However, correlation is not causation. While any program or intervention may contribute to an outcome, it is never the sole cause (Dimmit, Carey & Hatch, 2007).

EVALUATION AND IMPROVEMENT

Program evaluation and improvement has four components:
1. Self-analysis of the school counselors' strengths, areas of improvement related to knowledge, abilities and skills and attitudes necessary to meet the demands of the profession using the school counselor competencies assessment. (See School Counselor Competencies Assessment, p. 105.)
2. Self-analysis of the school counseling program's strengths and areas of improvement using the school counseling program assessment. (See School Counseling Program Assessment, p. 105.)
3. Evaluation of the school counselor's performance by an administrator using the school counselor performance appraisal. (See example of School Counselor Performance Appraisal, p. 112)
4. Review of program goals created at the beginning of the school year.

Analysis of School Counselor Competencies Assessment

The ASCA School Counselor Competencies (2007) were developed by a diverse group of practicing school counselors, district supervisors and counselor educators. The competencies were developed to align with the ASCA National Model and identify the knowledge, attitudes and skills required of a professional school counselor. These competencies have been identified as those that will best equip new and experienced school counselors with the skills to establish, maintain and enhance a comprehensive, developmental, results-based school counseling program that addresses academic achievement, career planning and personal/social development. (See School Counselor Competencies, p. 148.)

The ASCA School Counselor Competencies are provided in an assessment format and can be used in a variety of ways. School counselor education programs can use the competencies as benchmarks for training. Practicing school counselors could use them as a checklist to self-evaluate to make a professional development plan. School administrators may find these competencies useful as a guide for seeking and hiring competent school counselors and for developing meaningful school counselor performance evaluations.

Analysis of School Counseling Program Assessment

A comprehensive school counseling program is multifaceted and designed with continuous evaluation and modification in mind. The school counseling program assessment aligns with the four components of the ASCA National Model and serves as a tool for analyzing each component. (See School Counseling Program Assessment, p. 42.)

Each component includes the criteria for each subsection and includes benchmarks for program implementation. The primary purpose for collecting this information is to guide future actions within the program and to improve future results for students. The school counseling program assessment is used to identify gaps in the program and to identify goals for the next school year. The assessment has been written to be consistent with the Recognized ASCA Model Program (RAMP) application process and therefore could also be used as a tool to help a program evaluate its readiness to apply for RAMP status.

Assessment Criteria:
- No   the criterion is not in place
- In Progress   the criterion is being developed or implemented
- Yes   the criterion is in place or implemented

The school counseling program assessment is conducted annually, typically in the spring. After completing the assessment, analyze responses to determine the following:
- Strengths of the program
- Areas for improvement
- Short-range goals for improvement
- Long-range goals for improvement

Determining baseline data prior to programmatic restructuring provides necessary information for data-based decision making. Each year data are charted indicating growth or change in the areas of concern. The data are analyzed in relation to progress made toward the schoolwide mission and program goals. Noticing trends over time invites reflection, discussion and participation by all stakeholders in assessing the program for continual program evaluation and improvement.

The results of the program assessment drive program goals, training and behavior for the following year. Sharing the results with your administrator and advisory council can also be an effective method of educating key stakeholders about the impact a school counseling program can have on student success.

School Counselor Performance Appraisal

A School Counselor Performance Appraisal is an evaluation of the school counselor's performance. This appraisal is conducted once a year by an administrator. The appraisal document is frequently developed by school, district or state guidelines for school counselor evaluation, but it is recommended that the following criteria be considered in performance appraisal.

- The appraisal should contain three components: self-evaluation, administrative evaluation and assessment of goal attainment (Gysbers & Henderson, 2012).
- "Evaluators of school counselors' performance should be trained to understand school counselors' jobs and professional roles and in appropriate methods for gathering data to support evaluation" (Gysbers & Henderson, 2012, p. 355).

- Annual evaluation should use forms and tools specifically designed for school counselor performance evaluation.
- The school counselor performance standards from the ASCA National Model provide a sound framework for designing a school counselor evaluation.
- ASCA's School Counselor Competencies are an excellent resource for self-assessment or creating a school counselor performance evaluation form.

An example of the school counselor performance appraisal is offered (see p. 112). The example is based on the model provided by the North Carolina job description that identifies three major functions of the school counselor role: development and management of a comprehensive school counseling program, delivery of a comprehensive school counseling program and accountability and aligns with the ASCA School Counselor Competencies.

Program Goal Analysis

At the conclusion of the school year, as part of the program evaluation, the school counselor reviews the program goals identified in the beginning of the school year. It is likely the program goals were considered when developing the curriculum action plan, the small-group action plan and/or the closing-the-gap action plan. Review the results reports related to the program goals and consider implications for the school counseling program and future program goals.

Here are some questions to guide review of each of the program goals.
- Was the goal a SMART goal (specific, measurable, attainable, results-oriented and time-bound)?
- Was the goal a closing-the-gap goal?
- Was the goal met? If not, why not?
- What are the implications for goal setting for the following year?
- What implications do these results have for the school counseling program?

References

Dimmit, C. (2009). Why evaluation matters: Determining effective school counseling practices. *Professional School Counseling, 12*, 395-399.

Dimmitt, C., Carey, J., & Hatch, T. (2007). *Evidence-based school counseling: Making a difference with data-driven practices.* Thousand Oaks, CA: Corwin Press.

Gysbers, N. C., & Henderson, P. (2012). *Developing and managing your school guidance and counseling program* (5th ed.). Alexandria, VA: American Counseling Association.

Hatch, T., & Chen-Hayes, S. F. (2008). School counselor beliefs about ASCA model school counseling programs components using the SCPSC scale. *Professional School Counselor, 12*, 34-42.

Holcomb-McCoy, C. (2007). *School counselors to close the achievement gap: A social justice framework for success.* Thousand Oaks, CA: Corwin Press.

House, R. M., & Hayes, R. L. (2002). *School counselors becoming key players in educational reform.* Professional School Counseling, 5, 249-255.

Rowell, L. (2006). Action research and school counseling: Closing the gap between research and practice. *Professional School Counseling, 9*, 376-384.

Virginia School Counselor Association (2008). *Virginia professional school counseling program manual*. Yorktown, VA: Author.

Ward, C. (2009). *An examination of the impact of the ACAA National Model on student achievement at Recognized ASCA Program (RAMP) elementary schools*. Tex A&M University –Corpus Christi. DAI-A71/03.

Ware, W., & Galassi, J. (2006) Using correlational and prediction data to enhance student achievement in k-12 schools: A practical application for school counselors. *Professional School Counseling, 9,* 344-356.

Whiston, S. C., & Quinby, R. F. (2009). Review of school counseling outcome research. *Psychology in the Schools, 46(3),* 267 – 272.

Young, A., & Kaffenberger, C. (2009). *Making data work*. Alexandria, VA: American School Counselor Association.

Young, A., & Kaffenberger, C. (2011). The beliefs and practices of school counselor who use data to implement school counseling programs. *Professional School Counseling, 15,* 67-76.

Middle School Data Profile

Enrollment	2009-2010 #	2009-2010 %	2010-2011 #	2010-2011 %	2011-2012 #	2011-2012 %
Total enrollment	930	100	920	100	940	100
Gifted (school-based)	94	10.10	92	10.00	95	10.00
English for speakers of other languages	140	18.20	170	18.40	182	20.00
Special education services	119	12.20	120	13.00	125	13.1

Attendance Rate	2009-2010 %	2010-2011 %	2011-2012 %
All students	93	92	89
Asian or Pacific Islander	93	93	92
Black	91	90	90
Hispanic/Latino	89	89	87
White	95	95	94
Students with disabilities	91	91	90
Students identified as disadvantaged	91	90	87
Limited English proficiency students	92	91	89

Race/Ethnicity	2009-2010 #	2009-2010 %	2010-2011 #	2010-2011 %	2011-2012 #	2011-2012 %
Asian or Pacific Islander	146	15.70	152	14.34	165	17.50
Black	311	33.40	292	31.63	269	28.60
Hispanic/Latino	198	21.25	250	27.17	301	32.00
White	275	29.56	226	24.56	205	21.90

Students with Disabilities	2009-2010 #	2009-2010 %	2010-2011 #	2010-2011 %	2011-2012 #	2011-2012 %
All Students with disabilities	119	100.00	120	100.00	125	100.00
Asian or Pacific Islander	21	17.60	19	15.80	19	15.10
Black	35	29.30	37	30.80	43	34.30
Hispanic/Latino	42	35.30	40	30.00	42	34.20
White	21	17.60	24	19.00	21	15.20

Economically Disadvantaged	2009-2010 #	2009-2010 %	2010-2011 #	2010-2011 %	2011-2012 #	2011-2012 %
Yes	238	25.60	259	28.10	286	30.40

School Safety	2009-2010 #	2010-2011 #	2011-2012 #
Weapons offenses	6	5	8
Offenses against students	28	44	51
Offenses against staff	7	8	28
Alcohol, tobacco, drug offenses	5	4	9
Disorderly or disruptive behavior	184	198	249
Technology offenses	10	36	47

ACCOUNTABILITY

Middle School Data Profile

Percentage of Students Passing/Tested*	2009-2010		2010-2011		2011-2012	
	Passed	Tested	Passed	Tested	Passed	Tested
All students	73	100	74	100	73	100
Race/Ethnicity Asian or Pacific Islander	72	100	74	100	73	100
Black	69	99	71	99	71	99
Hispanic/Latino	67	99	71	99	69	99
White (not of Hispanic origin)	76	100	75	100	76	100
Students with disabilities	69	99	66	99	65	99
Students identified as disadvantaged	66	99	67	99	67	99
Limited English proficient students	70	98	74	99	72	98

Percentage English State Assessment Scores* 7th Grade	2009-2010		2010-2011		2011-2012	
	Passed	Tested	Passed	Tested	Passed	Tested
All students	74	100	73	100	71	100
Race/Ethnicity Asian or Pacific Islander	72	100	74	100	73	100
Black	69	99	70	99	70	99
Hispanic/Latino	67	99	67	99	69	99
White (not of Hispanic origin)	77	100	76	100	73	100
Students with disabilities	70	99	66	99	70	99
Students identified as disadvantaged	69	99	65	99	69	99
Limited English proficient students	74	99	64	99	65	99

Percentage Math State Assessment Scores* 8th Grade	2009-2010		2010-2011		2011-2012	
	Passed	Tested	Passed	Tested	Passed	Tested
All students	76	100	75	100	75	100
Race/Ethnicity Asian or Pacific Islander	80	100	81	100	82	100
Black	69	99	70	99	70	99
Hispanic/Latino	64	99	63	99	60	99
White (not of Hispanic origin)	77	100	76	100	75	100
Students with disabilities	70	100	66	99	70	99
Students identified as disadvantaged	69	99	65	99	70	99
Limited English proficient students	74	99	64	99	63	99

*Pass rate for state accreditation for seventh-grade English is 74 percent.
**Pass rate for state accreditation for eighth-grade math is 75 percent.
Special Features: Block schedule; mentoring program; annual career day; afterschool programs such as guitar club, art club, college partnership; homework achievers.

Review the report card data and consider the following questions:

1. What is working well at this school?

2. What concerns you about these data?

3. Does an achievement gap exist? Describe.

4. What additional information do you need?

5. What should you focus on? What data should you collect?

Examples of information that can be learned from reviewing the middle school data profile:

- The number of economically disadvantaged students has increased in 2009 from 238 to 286 in 2011, an increase of 20 percent.
- Attendance rates have decreased in all demographic categories. The attendance rate has fallen from 93 percent to 89 percent since 2009.
- There has been a demographic shift in three years. The percent of African-American students has decreased by about 13.5 percent. The percent of Hispanic students has increased by 52 percent, and the percent of white students has decreased by 25 percent.
- There has been an increase in school safety offenses in all categories. For instance technology offenses (i.e., cyberbullying) have increased from 10 to 47 offenses, an increase of 370 percent.

After reviewing the school data profile school counselors can address the following questions:

- What impact has the changing demographics had on the school climate, the state testing scores, attendance and safety issues at the school?
- Do the school counselors need to collect additional data to understand the issue?
- What can the school counselors do to have an impact on the state testing gaps?
- Is the staff at this school prepared to work with a changing population of students, and is there anything the school counselors can do to facilitate this transition?
- Do students at this school feel engaged? Do students believe the faculty is there to help them address problems?
- Can school counseling goals be identified that are related to this data analysis?

Adapted from:
Young, A., & Kaffenberger, C. (2009). *Making DATA work*. Alexandria, VA: American School Counselor Association.

ACCOUNTABILITY

School Counselor Performance Appraisal Template

Adapted from the North Carolina School Counselor Job Description

School Counselor_____ Date_____

Evaluator_____ Position_____

0	1	2	3
Unsatisfactory	Basic	Proficient	Distinguished

Duties and Responsibilities

DESCRIPTION	RATING
1. Major Function: Development and Management of a Comprehensive School Counseling Program	
1.1 Discusses the comprehensive school counseling program with the school administrator.	
1.2 Uses data to develop school counseling program goals, and shares the goals with stakeholders (i.e., administrators, teachers, students, parents, community and business leaders).	
1.3 Uses data to develop curriculum, small-group and closing-the-gap action plans for effective delivery of the school counseling program.	
1.4 Uses the majority of time providing direct and indirect student services through the school counseling core curriculum, individual student planning and responsive services and most of the remaining time in program management, system support and accountability. (Approximately 80 percent or more of time in direct and indirect services and 20 percent or less of time in program support.)	
1.5 Uses data to develop comprehensive programs that meet student needs.	
Observations and comments:	
2. Major Function: Delivery of a Comprehensive School Counseling Program	
Direct Services	
2.1 Provides direct student services (school counseling core curriculum, individual student planning and responsive services).	
2.2 Delivers school counseling core curriculum lessons in classroom and large-group settings.	
2.3 Provides appraisal and advisement to assist all students with academic, career and personal/social planning.	
2.4 Provides individual and group counseling to students with identified concerns and needs.	

DESCRIPTION	RATING
Indirect Services	
2.5 Indirect student services are provided on behalf of identified students; strategies to include referrals, consultation and collaboration.	
2.6 Refers students and parents to appropriate school and community resources to support student achievement and success.	
2.7 Consults with parents and other educators to share strategies that support student achievement and success.	
2.8 Collaborates with parents, other educators and community resources to support student achievement and success.	
Observations and comments:	
3. Major Function: Accountability	
3.1 Identifies and analyzes school data to inform the school counseling program and measure program results.	
3.2 Analyzes data on how time is used and adjusts program delivery to meet student needs as demonstrated in school data.	
3.3 Collects and analyzes results data of school counseling program activities to guide program evaluation and improvement.	
3.4 Monitors student academic performance, attendance and behavioral data to inform school counseling program goals.	
3.5 Conducts self-analysis to determine strengths and areas of improvement and plans professional development accordingly.	
3.6 Conducts a school counseling program assessment annually to review extent of program implementation and effectiveness.	
3.7 Shares school counseling program results data with relevant stakeholders.	
Observations and comments:	
Total Score	
Average Score	

ACCOUNTABILITY

Overall Performance Comments by Evaluator:

Comments by School Counselor:

_____   _____

School Counselor   Date   Evaluator   Date

SCHOOL COUNSELING CORE CURRICULUM RESULTS REPORT

Goal: _____   Year: _____

Lessons and Activities Related to Goal:

Grade Level	Lesson Topic	Lesson Will Be Presented In Which Class/Subject	ASCA Domain, Standard and Competency	Curriculum and Materials	Start/End	Process Data (Number of students affected)	Perception Data (Surveys or assessments used)	Outcome Data (Achievement, attendance and/or behavior data)	Implications

SMALL-GROUP RESULTS REPORT

_____ Year: _____
(School Name)

Group Name: _____

Goal: _____

Target Group: _____

Data Used to Identify Students: _____

School Counselor(s)	ASCA Domain, Standard and Student Competency	Outline of Group Sessions to be Delivered	Resources Needed	Process Data (Number of students affected)	Perception Data (Data from surveys used)	Outcome Data (Achievement, attendance and/or behavior data collected)	Implications

CLOSING-THE-GAP RESULTS REPORT

Year: _____

_____
(School Name)

Goal: _____

Target Group: _____

Data Used to Identify Students: _____

School Counselor(s)	ASCA Domain, Standard and Student Competency	Type of Activities to be Delivered in What Manner?	Resources Needed	Process Data (Number of students affected)	Perception Data (Data from surveys used)	Outcome Data (Achievement, attendance and/or behavior data collected)	Implications

WHAT DOES IT MEAN TO HAVE A DATA-DRIVEN SCHOOL COUNSELING PROGRAM?

By Carol Kaffenberger, Ph.D., Associate Professor Emerita, George Mason University

A school counselor has been implementing a peer mediation program at her school for three years but has not collected data to evaluate its effectiveness. Without data she can only hope that the program is effective.

Having a data-driven school counseling program means that at each stage of program delivery and assessment, data are used to inform the decisions that are made. Data identify the population of students in need of an intervention. Data drive decisions about the goals of the intervention. Data measure the effectiveness of the intervention. In addition to the use of data to drive program decisions, data are also used to monitor student achievement and demonstrate the impact the school counseling program is having on students. Systemic change does not occur without collecting and examining data to understand the cause of the issue or the gap.

How does this work in practice? Initially it means reviewing existing data to determine what services are needed to address opportunity or achievement gaps. You could conduct this review of existing data by examining the school data profile, looking for achievement, opportunity or attainment gaps. Consider what the changes or gaps mean for the school counseling program and how school counseling interventions could contribute to closing the gaps.

Data can also be useful in understanding an issue. Collecting data before determining what intervention is needed will contribute to understanding underlying issues. For example, you may be concerned about bullying at your school. Collecting perception data from students or faculty may point to an intervention that is targeted and focused on addressing the issue. At one middle school, survey data indicated students were aware of the skills for handling bullying but didn't report bullying because they didn't believe the staff would take action. In this case implementing a schoolwide educational program aimed at the adults in the building would be more effective than classroom lessons on what to do about bullying.

Once you've implemented an intervention, you'll use data to determine whether it was effective. Perception data shows you whether you've achieved the goals of the intervention and whether the students believe they have benefited. This may mean collecting perception data such as pre- and post test scores before and after delivering the intervention. Do the students believe their knowledge has increased as a result of the lesson? Outcome data measure the impact of the intervention on students and indicate whether there has been a change in achievement, attendance or behavior scores. Outcome data are the most powerful.

Here is an example of you can use data to create systemic change. A middle school counseling team was worried about the growing number of students with D/F grades in spite of the use of a variety of traditional student-focused interventions, such as student and parent conferences, homework club and mentoring. In reviewing the school data they noticed the attendance rate for the school had fallen three years in a row, and discipline incidents had sharply increased. Something had changed at this school.

By examining the data they realized the demographics at the school had changed too. Before implementing strategies to address these issues, the school counselors decided to collect data to understand underlying factors that might be contributing to the issues at their school. They collected data in two ways. With permission from the administrators they conducted a six-question online survey with students who had one or more D/F grade. They also decided to conduct a focus group with a select group of the parents of students with D/F grades to hear what they had to say. Survey results indicated that students did not think coming to school was important; they were unsure about whether high school graduation was important. Furthermore, they indicated they didn't believe there was teacher/staff member they could go to for help. Clearly, this group of students was not engaged in this school community.

The school counselors took the data to the administration and the staff for discussion. What resulted was a schoolwide examination of the school culture, which revealed that other students were not feeling a part of the school community. The faculty as a group discussed schoolwide strategies to create a more positive culture in the school and requested professional development to help them work more effectively with students with poor grades. Other interventions included changes in policy around attendance, admittance in advanced courses, small-group counseling focusing not only on study skills but also on career and college readiness. Parent interventions including parent workshops held in the community and efforts to build community alliances. Addressing barriers to student success created a culture of change at this school and is an example of how data can be used to drive program improvement.

Steps to consider when implementing a data-driven school counseling program:
- Review school data reports over time to observe trends, changes and gaps.
- Consider how school counseling program goals align with the school mission statement and school improvement plan.
- Collect pre- and post-test data from school counseling lessons, group counseling, workshops and programs.

- Evaluate school counseling services and programs to determine what impact they are having on student success and how they can be improved or if they should be eliminated.
- Conduct a program assessment once a year.
- Use evidence-based school counseling interventions.
- Set measurable attainable school counseling goals.
- Share data with stakeholders.
- Consider how the data you are examining, collecting and sharing measure student success.

COLLECTING AND SHARING RESULTS IN AN ARTICLE

By Christopher Sink, Ph.D., Professor, Seattle Pacific University

In response to the longstanding input of school counseling leaders, the ASCA National Model encourages school counselors to be accountable for their work with students, staff and parents/caregivers. Across the country, school counselors are following this recommendation by informally and formally measuring student outcomes in the academic, personal/social and career developmental domains. Accountability evidence can be drawn from multiple sources, including participant data collected before and after facilitating classroom guidance activities, individual counseling meetings and small-group sessions. School- or district-generated student attendance records and disciplinary referrals are available for reporting as well. With this information school counselors can then document positive student outcomes by using spreadsheet software and its various tools to create summary tables and charts.

Regrettably many school counselors still aren't convinced data collection is an indispensable professional activity, while others just need some assistance to competently respond to questions such as, "I've done some innovative things in my building, but how do I use data to document their usefulness? What should I do with all this data? How do I share my good ideas with my colleagues?"

One effective way to share your data is to write an article about your work. Here are some tips to follow:

Select a poignant topic. Finding a meaningful and timely subject to write about is one of the keys to success. Do some background reading to help frame your writing project (e.g., *ASCA School Counselor* and *Professional School Counseling*). Start with reviewing articles published in school-counseling-related journals and magazines. These can provide both inspiration and foundational information. The ASCA National Model and online searches can yield additional ideas. If you want to write a results-based article, pick a topic you already have some outcome data on or could readily obtain the information. For instance, report on the promising student outcome data obtained from an eight-week anti-bullying program you instituted.

Other more obvious recommendations to consider as you launch into this work bear repeating: (a) ask for ideas and writing support from your colleagues and from school counselor educators at a nearby university; (b) avoid topics that already inundate the school counseling literature; and (c) select a topic or theme you have some expertise in.

Decide on a publication outlet that will be receptive to your article. Should you want to publish your manuscript in a school-counseling-related journal, magazine or newsletter, there are multiple options to consider. For example, ASCA and its state associations have several options. At the national level, consider writing a piece for *ASCA School Counselor* magazine or *Professional School Counseling* journal. State school counseling publications are largely practitioner-focused and actively seeking contributors. Carefully read the author guidelines summarized on the publication's Web site, and make sure your topic fits within the publication's major areas of interest. Do not be afraid to contact the publication's editor for additional information and assistance. It is important to note that the writing quality and research rigor varies with the scholarly level of the publication. Begin with writing a piece for a magazine or newsletter, and then move to a professional journal if you have a substantial work to disseminate.

Formulate a research and writing plan. Once you have decided on a timely and appropriate topic and a couple of viable publishing options, develop a brief research and writing plan to serve as a roadmap. Include at least these items:
- Determine what sources of information (background literature and data sources) you have and those you may still need. For example, review already published research articles on the efficacy of bullying programs; calculate the number of students referred to the school's office for disciplinary reasons related to bullying; examine pre-and post-test data obtained from the anti-bullying/victimization classroom intervention; obtain interview and observational data from program participants.
- When you are using student data for your article, ensure that no identifying information is included in the narrative. Obtain written parental consent for all research studies you intend to disseminate. Hopefully you can ask a district-level research or assessment manager for assistance in this area.
- Set a realistic timeline for when you want to submit the article for publication, and then set smaller writing goals along the way.
- Ask a colleague who is a good writer or a school counselor educator to serve as your supplemental "editor." Have that person read your drafts and provide honest feedback.
- If you need assistance with data analysis and report writing, again consult a district-level research or assessment manager to lend a hand or partner with a school counselor educator as well.

Implement your writing plan. Perseverance is essential. Just like a diet, writing an article provides delayed gratification. Submit drafts to your editor, and stick to the timeline. Sometimes it takes three to five drafts before you're ready to submit your article.

Submit your article to a publishing venue. Make sure the article is free of errors and formatting problems. Most publication sources in school counseling require the careful use of the American Psychological Association's formatting and writing style, now in its sixth edition (often called the "APA Style Manual" for short). Include a brief cover letter addressed to the publication editor. Include the proposed title of the paper, a rationale for the article's foci and why it is germane to the publication. Also add your contact information. The APA Style Manual provides a sample letter.

Be aware that most article submissions, whether they are intended for professional magazines, newsletters or journals, go through some type of review process, and this may take up to three months. The response from the editor is generally a formal correspondence indicating both the manuscript's strengths and limitations. If the editor thinks the document is publishable, the correspondence will also provide helpful recommendations to improve the quality of the manuscript. Plan on revising the article, perhaps two or three times, before it is ready to go to press. Should you receive an unfavorable response from the editor, try not to take it personally. In this case, rework the manuscript based on the feedback and resubmit to another related publishing source.

The writing process can be challenging, but it is certainly worth the effort. Your school counseling colleagues will appreciate hearing a strong voice from the field and learning from your work. Ultimately, students will benefit from your insights as well.

SCHOOL COUNSELOR EVALUATION

By Judy Bowers, Ed.D., Retired Coordinator of the School Counseling Program, Tucson Unified School District, Tucson, Ariz., and C:3 Counseling Grant Project Director

Since the ASCA National Model was first published in 2003, school counselors have expressed a desire to have a school counselor job description and evaluation reflecting the ASCA National Model. For many years in many states, school counselors were evaluated on several different evaluation forms, such as a teacher evaluation, an evaluation used for "other certified personnel," an evaluation for the social worker or psychologists or a form for resource personnel not teaching in the classroom. These evaluation forms were problematic as they did not specifically reflect the school counselor's unique job.

School counselors need an evaluation that is specific to school counseling because the role of the school counselor is unique and important. A typical evaluation could include four major functions of a school counseling program.

Development and management: School counselors are responsible for developing their school counseling program for all students and for managing it to show results.

Implementation: School counselors now work with all students to deliver a program reflecting the competencies in academic, career and personal/social domains. Programs are delivered in classrooms, in small groups or individually.

Accountability: In addition, school counselors are responsible for collecting and evaluating data showing results of their school counseling program. They are data experts in schools.

Systemic change agent: School counselors use their skills of leadership, advocacy and collaboration to work as systemic change agents for students.

Therefore, a school counselor evaluation needs to be coordinated with a school counselor job description specifically following the ASCA National Model.

ACCOUNTABILITY

In the accountability section of the ASCA National Model, school counselors are introduced to a sample performance appraisal instrument that accurately reflects the unique training of school counselors and their responsibilities within the school system. The performance appraisal can be an important tool in the school counselor's self-evaluation and a guide to personal and professional development planning.

When school counselors follow the ASCA National Model and fully implement all of the elements, they are also working at the distinguished level, or highest level, of a performance appraisal. School counselors should go through the ASCA program assessment yearly and check where they are regarding the implementation of all the elements and the criteria. This self-assessment helps school counselors understand what areas to focus on to improve their programs. It is easy to see that when school counselors implement the ASCA National Model, they are also doing their job to the fullest extent.

Some district and state school counselor performance appraisals list suggested artifacts to show an element is being implemented. An example from the sample performance appraisal instrument is major function one – development and management of a comprehensive school counseling program. Artifacts for this function could include classroom lessons, a master calendar, program goals, closing-the-gap action plans and the curriculum action plan. By including the artifacts with the criteria for each level of school counselor implementation from unsatisfactory through distinguished, an evaluator will be able to understand what a fully implemented school counseling program includes.

Performance appraisal instruments specific to school counseling positively reflect the school counselor's unique role in today's schools. It is an important tool in program implementation, self-evaluation and planning for professional development.

Where To Start

When implementing the ASCA National Model, consider the steps below to help manage the transition to a comprehensive school counseling program.

1. Read or review the ASCA National Model.
2. Communicate your intent to implement the ASCA National Model with school and district administrators.
3. Use the program assessment to compare your current program with the ASCA National Model.
4. Identify areas of strength and areas to improve based on the results of the program assessment.
5. Review the school's academic, attendance and behavioral data.
6. Prioritize areas to improve based on school data.
7. Identify assessments and tools in the management component that correspond to the areas to improve.
8. Identify collaborators needed for implementation.
9. Develop a one-to-three-year plan for implementation of the foundation, management, delivery and accountability components, including a timeline and persons responsible for each item in the plan.
10. Present plan to administrators.
11. Implement the plan, and collect data on program implementation using the tools in the management component.
12. Analyze data collected to determine the results of the program following suggestions in the accountability component.
13. Share your results with school and district staff.
14. Complete and analyze the program assessment each year to compare your program with the ASCA National Model.
15. After implementation, consider applying for the Recognized ASCA Model Program (RAMP) designation to show how your program makes a difference in student achievement and success.

Appendix

Changes in the Third Edition of the ASCA National Model

The following information provides a brief synopsis of the changes made in the third edition of "The ASCA National Model: A Framework for School Counseling Programs."

Themes
The themes of the third edition are the same as the second edition. Additional information has been included, such as special topics written by professionals in the field, and the themes have been woven throughout the four components.

1. Leadership
2. Advocacy
3. Collaboration
4. Systemic Change

Foundation
This section addresses components that drive every school counseling program.

The third edition includes three sections:
1. Program Focus
2. Student Competencies
3. Professional Competencies

The content from the second edition is aligned under the new sections, and additional topics have been added, including special topics written by professionals in the field related to specific sections.

Second Edition Topics	Third Edition	
	Section	Topics
Beliefs and Philosophy	**Program Focus**	**Beliefs and Vision Statement** "Beliefs and Philosophy" has been divided into separate sections of beliefs and vision in alignment with language used by education leaders, schools and districts. Research studies for school improvement, leadership and change name vision as a key factor in organizational effectiveness. Components of the beliefs and philosophy section have been maintained within either the beliefs or vision sections.
Mission Statement	**Program Focus**	**Mission Statement** No significant changes.
		Program Goals (New) Research studies for school improvement, leadership and change name vision, mission and goals as key factors in organizational effectiveness. Although the second edition of the ASCA National Model encouraged goal setting through action plans, the third edition increases the focus of goal setting through the use of data.
ASCA Standards for Student Academic, Career and Personal/ Social Development	**Student Competencies**	**ASCA Student Standards** Titled "ASCA National Standards" in the second edition, the title of these standards was changed to reflect the focus on students. The standards have not changed.
		Other Student Standards (New) School counselors are encouraged to consider how other student standards complement and inform their comprehensive school counseling program. This section helps school counselors demonstrate how their program aligns with other standards that are important to state and district initiatives as appropriate (e.g., state standards, 21st Century, Character Ed).
	Professional Competencies	**ASCA School Counselor Competencies (New)** These competencies, developed several years after the release of the second edition of the ASCA National Model, outline the knowledge, attitudes and skills that ensure school counselors are equipped to meet the rigorous demands of the profession and the needs of preK-12 students. The competencies also serve as a guide for professional development.
		ASCA Ethical Standards for School Counselors (New) This essential document is now included in the Foundation.

Management

This component provides assessments and tools to manage a school counseling program, including planning, implementation and data collection.

The management component in the third edition includes new and revised tools designed to help develop and maintain program components as well as special topics written by professionals in the field related to specific sections. School counselors can use and adapt the assessments and tools as needed to continue to improve their school counseling program.

Second Edition Topics	Third Edition	
	Section	Topics
Topics	Assessments	**School Counselor Competencies Assessment (New)** This assessment is based on the ASCA School Counselor Competencies. It is designed to help school counselors identify knowledge, abilities and skills and attitudes that meet the rigorous demands of the profession.
	Assessments	**School Counseling Program Assessment (Revised)** This assessment was titled "Program Audit" in the second edition. Language has been changed from audit to assessment as audit implies an outside auditor, and assessment implies an internal review. The criteria have been condensed and streamlined.
Use of Time	Assessments	**Use-of-Time Assessment (New)** This assessment was created to help school counselors analyze their use of time in ▪ Direct and indirect student services (80 percent or more) ▪ Program management and school support (20 percent or less). Program management includes foundation, management, accountability tasks and fair-share responsibilities)
Management Agreements	Tools	**Annual Agreement** This agreement was titled "management agreement" in the second edition. The title has changed to emphasize that the agreement is completed each year. Professional development and fair-share responsibilities are included in this document.
Advisory Council	Tools	**Advisory Council** Additional direction and information have been included.
Use of Data	Tools	**School Data Profile (New)** The school data profile informs school counseling goals and may identify a need for systemic change. This tool is designed to help school counselors track achievement, attendance, behavior and school safety data to identify gaps. Program results data are categorized as process, perception and outcome (called "results" in the second edition) data. Data for this document are frequently pulled from existing data sources or student information systems at the school.

Second Edition Topics	Third Edition	
	Section	Topics
Action Plans	Tools	**Action Plans** ▪ Curriculum Action Plan ▪ Small-Group Action Plans (New) ▪ Closing-the-Gap Action Plans The small-group action plan template was created and aligned with the curriculum and closing-the-gap action plans to increase the focus on small groups. This plan will help school counselors organize and collect data for small groups.
		Lesson Plans (New) This template was designed to help school counselors in the development and implementation of classroom activities.
Calendars	Tools	**Annual Calendar Template** **Weekly Calendar Template** No significant changes.

Delivery

This component focuses on the method of implementing the school counseling program to students.

The third edition draws a clear distinction between direct and indirect student services. The components of the delivery system are divided between direct and indirect student services, all of which are part of the second edition. Some system support topics from the second edition of the delivery system have been moved to the other components as noted below.

Second Edition Topics	Third Edition			
	Section	Topics		
Guidance Curriculum **Individual Student Planning** **Responsive Services**	**Direct Student Services**	In-person interactions between school counselors and students		
		Elements and Strategies	**Recipient**	**Method**
		School Counseling Core Curriculum ▪ Instruction ▪ Group Activities Individual Student Planning ▪ Appraisal ▪ Advisement Responsive Services ▪ Counseling ▪ Crisis Response	All Students DATA DRIVEN Identified Students	Interactions with Students in: ▪ Large Group ▪ Classroom ▪ Small Group ▪ Individual

Second Edition Topics	Third Edition			
	Section	Topics		
Guidance Curriculum **Individual Student Planning** **Responsive Services**	**Indirect Student Services**	Services provided on behalf of students as a result of the school counselor's interactions with others.		
		Elements and Strategies	**Recipient**	**Method**
		▪ Referrals ▪ Consultation ▪ Collaboration	All Students DATA DRIVEN Identified Students	Interactions with Others
System Support		**Included in other components** ▪ Program management and operations are included in the management component. ▪ Professional development is included in the foundation and management component. ▪ Data analysis is included in the accountability component.		

Accountability

This component is designed to help school counselors analyze data collected from other sections of the ASCA National Model.

The third edition includes three subsections:

1. **Data Analysis** – Helps school counselors analyze data that inform decisions about the school counseling program. The data analyzed have been collected over time and inform school counselors about student needs and school and community trends.
2. **Program Results** – Help school counselors create curriculum, small-group and closing-the-gap results reports.
3. **Evaluation and Improvement** – Help school counselors analyze self-assessment and program assessment data to identify strengths and areas of improvement.

Second Edition Topics	Third Edition	
	Section	Topics
Results Reports	**Data Analysis**	**School Data Profile Analysis (New)** Tips for analyzing process, perception and outcome (called "results" in second edition) data are included. Analysis of the school data profile informs school counseling goals and may identify a need for systemic change. The analysis helps school counselors track achievement, attendance, behavior and school safety data to identify gaps.

Second Edition Topics	Third Edition	
	Section	Topics
Results Reports	Data Analysis	**Use-of-Time Analysis (New)** Tips for analyzing the use-of-time template are presented. The analysis informs program decisions about how to best meet student needs in the future.
	Program Results	**Curriculum Results Report Analysis** Tips are presented for analyzing data collected from classroom and large-group presentations.
		Small-Group Results Report Analysis (New) Tips are presented for analyzing data collected from small-group counseling activities.
	Evaluation and Improvement	**School Counselor Competencies Assessment Analysis (New)** Tips are presented for analyzing this self-assessment.
Program Audit	Evaluation and Improvement	**Program Assessment Analysis (Revised)** Tips are presented for analyzing the program assessment.
School Counselor Performance Standards	Evaluation and Improvement	**School Counseling Performance Appraisal Template (New)** A template for school counselor performance appraisal is presented.
		Program Goal Analysis (New) Direction for analyzing progress toward program goals has been included.

Index of Special Topics

Use-of-Time Comparison for Delivery of the School Counseling Program

The third edition of the ASCA National Model offers schools increased flexibility in determining how time is distributed in each element of the delivery component. Although spending 80 percent of time in direct and indirect student services is the general recommendation for a comprehensive school counseling program, use of time within the 80 percent may be allocated differently from school to school based on needs identified in school data. All components of direct and indirect student services are necessary for a program to be considered a comprehensive school counseling program, but decisions about time allocation are based on student needs as demonstrated in the school data profile and alignment with school and school counseling program goals.

School counselors may find it necessary to adjust the percentage of time in each of the delivery categories from year to year to meet students' needs. In addition, school counselors are able to justify their modification to the suggested use of time by providing a rationale for an increase or decrease to any category based on research and best practice. In programs with more than one school counselor per site, there can be flexibility between and among school counselors in determining how much time individual school counselors spend in the delivery components.

ASCA National Model (third edition) Delivery	K-12	ASCA National Model (second edition) Delivery	Elementary	Middle	Secondary
Direct Student Services ◻ School Counseling Core Curriculum ◻ Individual Student Planning ◻ Responsive Services **Indirect Student Services** ◻ Referrals ◻ Consultation ◻ Collaboration	80% or more	**Guidance Curriculum**	35%-45%	25%-35%	15%-25%
		Individual Student Planning	5%-10%	15%-25%	25%-35%
		Responsive Services	30%-40%	30%-40%	25%-35%
		System Support	10%-15%	10%-15%	15%-20%

Adapted from Gysbers, N.C. & Henderson, P. (2012) *Developing and managing your school counseling program* (5th ed.), Alexandria, VA: American Counseling Association.

Included in Other Components

Program Planning and School Support ▪ Program management and operations (management) ▪ Professional development (foundation and management) ▪ Data analysis (accountability) ▪ Fair-share responsibilities (management)	20% or less

Fundamental Questions and Principles from the Theory Behind the ASCA National Model

By Patricia Henderson, Ed.D.

The information below describes the theory base supporting the ASCA National Model. Seven fundamental questions are identified as those needing to be answered in a school counseling theory. For each question, answers from the ASCA Ethical Standards for School Counselors, from the profession's history and from the school counseling effectiveness research base are provided. These sources support the 27 major principles identified as the answers to the seven questions. Each principle is supported by the profession's values, history and research. The ASCA National Model rests on these principles.

For additional information, including historical roots and research supporting these principles, see the full document at *www.ASCANationalModel.org*.

Fundamental Questions	ASCA National Model Principles
1. What do students need that the school counseling profession, based on its special body of knowledge, can best address?	**Principle 1:** As with other dimensions of their development, all students benefit from assistance in accomplishing the age-appropriate tasks related to their academic, career and personal/social development.

Fundamental Questions	ASCA National Model Principles
2. Which students benefit from activities designed to address these needs?	**Principle 2:** All students can benefit from interventions designed to assist their academic, career and personal/social development.
	Principle 3: Some students need more assistance in accomplishing the age-appropriate academic, career and personal/social developmental tasks. These students benefit from preventive or remedial interventions specially designed to help them achieve tasks appropriate to their developmental level.
3. What are school counselors best qualified to do to help students?	**Principle 4:** School counselors are qualified to make contributions to all students' development in the areas of academic (educational), career and personal/social development.
	Principle 5: School counselors can design and deliver interventions to meet students' developmental needs and to meet students' needs for prevention and remediation, thereby helping to close gaps between specific groups of students and their peers.
	Principle 6: School counselors' interventions in students' academic, career and personal/social development help students acquire and apply knowledge, skills and attitudes promoting development in those three dimensions of human growth.
	Principle 7: School counselors can help other adults enhance their work with students' academic/educational, career and personal-social development and for the purpose of removing barriers to individual students' success.
4. How does school counseling relate to the overall educational program?	**Principle 8:** School counselors work with others in the school on behalf of students to support accomplishment of the school's mission and to assist in the removal of systemic barriers to student success.
5. How can school counseling be provided most effectively and efficiently?	**Principle 9:** The work of school counselors should be organized as a program.
	Principle 10: The delivery component dividing program activities into program components of direct services (school counseling core curriculum, individual student planning and responsive services) and indirect services (referrals, consultation and collaboration) is the most effective and efficient means for organizing the program.

Fundamental Questions	ASCA National Model Principles
5. How can school counseling be provided most effectively and efficiently?	**Principle 11:** The elements and strategies described as the delivery component for the school counseling program include all the means to have an impact on students' academic, career and personal/social development: direct student services (school counseling core curriculum, individual student planning and responsive services) and indirect student services (referrals, consultation and collaboration).
	Principle 12: School counseling program activities can be designed that positively affect all students' academic, career and personal/social development and that help those students whose healthy academic, career and/or personal/social development is threatened or interrupted.
	Principle 13: Intentionally designed interventions targeting identified needs or specified goals and objectives are more effective than interventions that are not intentionally designed.
6. How is a good school counseling program developed by a school?	**Principle 14:** A systematic approach to developing the school counseling program (i.e., planning and building the foundation, designing the delivery, managing the program, holding program staff accountable and evaluating the program) ensures its effectiveness and relevancy.
	Principle 15: Collaborative, cooperative planning with parents/guardians, teachers, administrators, staff and community members in developing a school counseling program results in the program being effective and an integral part of the total school mission.
	Principle 16: Effective school counseling programs are designed with awareness of local demographics and on student needs based on locally gathered data.
	Principle 17: Establishing priorities for and recognizing parameters within the program are critical to effective management and implementation of school counseling programs.
	Principle 18: There are organizational procedures school counselors can use to manage implementation of their programs for effectiveness, efficiency and relevancy to the school.
	Principle 19: Accountability for student results, school counselor performance and program completeness is essential to ensuring the effectiveness and relevance of school counseling programs, and it requires the collection and use of data.

Fundamental Questions	ASCA National Model Principles
6. How is a good school counseling program developed by a school?	**Principle 20:** Leadership for school counseling programs is a shared responsibility between school counselors and school principals.
7. How are the results of school counselors' work measured?	**Principle 21:** Having benefited from school counselors' interventions, students are more ready to learn academically and to be successful in school.
	Principle 22: Explicit statements of the results desired for students better ensure the achievement of those results.
	Principle 23: Evaluation of student results, school counselor performance and program completeness is essential to ensuring the effectiveness and relevance of school counseling programs, and it requires the collection and use of data.
	Principle 24: Evaluation of student results is based on established standards for the measurement of student development, growth and change.
	Principle 25: Evaluation of school counselors' performance is based on the appropriate role of the school counselor.
	Principle 26: Evaluation of program completeness is based on alignment with the ASCA National Model and the local program design.
	Principle 27: The purpose of evaluation is improvement.

Adapted from Henderson, P. (2005). The theory behind the ASCA national model. In *The ASCA National Model: A Framework for School Counseling* (2nd ed.). Alexandria, VA.

Glossary

Annual agreement: outlines the organization and focus of the school counseling program and is made between each school counselor and the administrator in charge of the school counseling program each school year.

Annual calendar: a calendar of school counseling program activities maintained by the school counseling staff and distributed to teachers, students and parents.

Data-driven: decisions concerning future action that are based on information, survey reports, assessments, statistics or other forms of data.

Delivery: the means around which the school counseling program is organized and delivered, including direct student services (school counseling core curriculum, individual student planning and responsive services) and indirect student services (referrals, consultation and collaboration).

Disaggregated data: data separated into component parts by specific variables such as ethnicity, gender and socioeconomic status.

Domains: broad areas of knowledge base (academic, career and personal/social) that promote and enhance the learning process.

Evaluation: a process used by an individual or group to determine progress or quality; evaluation is a key element in any improvement process.

Foundation: includes program focus, student competencies and professional competencies.

School counseling core curriculum: consists of structured developmental lessons designed to assist students in attaining the competencies from the ASCA Student Standards and is presented systematically through classroom and group activities K-12.

Non- school-counseling activity: any activity or duty not related to the development, implementation or evaluation of the school counseling program.

Indicator: measurable evidence that individuals have the knowledge, abilities or skills for a specific competency.

Individual student planning: ongoing systemic activities designed to assist the individual student in establishing personal goals and developing future plans, such as individual learning plans and graduation plans.

Leadership: capacity or ability to guide others; school counselors use leadership skills in their department and in their advocacy role.

Management: addresses the organization and allocation of resources to best address the goals of the school counseling program.

Mission statement: provides the focus and direction of the comprehensive school counseling program and aligns with the school's mission.

Outcome data: how students are measurably different as a result of the school counseling program.

Outcomes: demonstration of learning, performance or behavioral change after participating in the school counseling program.

Perception data: measure what students and others observe or perceive, knowledge gained, attitudes and beliefs held or competencies attained.

Performance appraisal: assessment of agreed-upon goals, contributions to the school counseling program, and personal and professional characteristics. Specifies contract status recommendations and indicates summative evaluation of school counselor effectiveness.

Personal/social development: maximizing each student's individual growth and social maturity in the areas of personal management and social interaction.

Process data: method of evaluation using figures to show the activities, rather than the results from the activities, such as numbers of students served, groups and classroom visits.

Program goals: define how the vision and mission will be accomplished and guide the development of curriculum, small-group and closing-the-gap action plans.

Professionalism: adherence to ethical, legal and professional standards developed by state and national school counseling organizations.

Program: A coherent sequence of instruction based upon a validated set of competencies.

Program assessment: assessment of the school counseling program on the components of the ASCA National Model; the primary purpose for completing the assessment is to guide future action within the program and to improve future results for students.

Program management: activities that develop, monitor and evaluate the implementation of the comprehensive school counseling program.

Responsive services: activities that meet students' immediate needs and concerns.

Results report: written presentation of the outcomes of counseling program activities; contains process, perception and outcome data.

Standards: the ASCA National Model addresses four types of standards. They are content standards, program standards, performance standards and ethical standards. Standards are statements of what should be done in each area.

Student success: a broad term for student achievement.

Systemic change: Change affecting the entire system; transformational; change affecting more than an individual or series of individuals; focus of the change is upon the dynamic of the environment, not the individual.

Use of data: the use of data to effect change within the school system is essential to ensure all students receive the benefits of a school counseling program.

References

American School Counselor Association (2006). The professional school counselor and equity for all students. *Position Statements*. Alexandria, VA: Author.

American School Counselor Association (2007). School counselor competencies. Alexandria, VA: Author.

American School Counselor Association (2009). The professional school counselor and student mental health. *Position Statements*. Alexandria, VA: Author.

American School Counselor Association. (2010). Ethical standards for school counselors. Alexandria, VA: Author.

Anderson, B. (1993). The stages of systemic change. *Educational Leadership, 51*, 14-17.

Bauman, S. (2004). School counselors and research revisited. *Professional School Counseling, 7*, 141-151.

Bolman, L. G., and Deal, T. E. (2008). *Reframing Organizations: Artistry, Choice and Leadership* (4th ed.). San Francisco: Jossey-Bass.

Campbell, C. A. & Dahir, C. A. (1997). *Sharing the vision: The national standards for school counseling programs*. Alexandria, VA: American School Counselor Association.

Corey, G., Corey, M. S., & Callanan, P. (2010). *Issues and ethics in the helping profession*. Pacific Grove, CA: Brooks/Cole.

Dahir, C. A., & Stone, C. B. (2012). *The transformed school counselor* (2nd ed.). Belmont, CA: Brooks/Cole.

Dahir, C. A. and Stone, C. B. (2009) School counselor accountability: The path to social justice and systemic change. *Journal of Counseling and Development, 87*, 12-20.

Dimmit, C. (2009). Why evaluation matters: Determining effective school counseling practices. *Professional School Counseling, 12*, 395-399.

Dimmitt, C., Carey, J. C. & Hatch, T. (2007). *Evidence-based school counseling: Making a difference with data-driven practices*. Thousand Oaks, CA: Corwin Press.

Dollarhide, C. T. (2003) School counselors as program leaders: Applying leadership contexts to school counseling. *Professional School Counseling, 6*, 304-308.

Dollarhide, C. T. & Saginak, K. A. (2012). *Comprehensive school counseling programs: K-12 delivery systems in action* (2nd ed.). Upper Saddle River, NJ: Pearson Education, Inc.

Doran, G. T. (1981). There's a S.M.A.R.T. way to write management's goals and objectives. *Management Review, 70*(11), 35-36.

DuFour, R., Eaker, R., Karhanek, G., & DuFour, R., (2004). *Whatever it takes: How professional learning communities respond when students don't learn.* Bloomington: Solution Tree.

Gysbers, N. C. & Henderson, P. (2012) *Developing and managing your school counseling program* (5th ed.). Alexandria, VA: American Counseling Association.

Hatch, T., & Chen-Hayes, S. F. (2008). School counselor beliefs about ASCA model school counseling programs components using the SCPSC scale. *Professional School Counseling, 12,* 34-42.

Haycock, K. (2001). Closing the achievement gap. *Educational Leadership, 58,* 6-11.

Holcomb-McCoy, C. (2007). *School counselors to close the achievement gap: A social justice framework for success.* Thousand Oaks, CA: Corwin Press.

House, R. M., & Hayes, R. L. (2002). School counselors becoming key players in educational reform. *Professional School Counseling, 5,* 249-255.

Johnson, C. D. & Johnson, S. K. (2001) *Results-based student support programs: Leadership academy workbook.* San Juan Capistrano, CA: Professional Update.

Jones, K. A., Jones, J., & Vermette, P. J. (2011). Six common lesson planning pitfalls: Recommendations for novice educators. *Education, 131,* 845-64.

Krathwohl, D. R. (2002). *A revision of Bloom's taxonomy: An overview.* Theory into Practice, 41, 213-218.

Kose, B.W. (2011). Developing a transformative school vision: Lessons from peer-nominated principals. *Education and Urban Society, 43,* 119-136.

Lawson, H. A. (2003). *Pursuing and securing collaboration to improve results. 102nd Yearbook of the National Society for the Study of Education.* Chicago: University of Chicago Press.

Leithwood, K., & Hallinger, P. (Senior Co-eds.; 2002). *The second international handbook of educational leadership and administration.* Dordrecht, Netherlands: Kluwer Press.

Levin, I. M. (2000). Vision revisited: Telling the story of the future. *The Journal of Applied Behavioral Science, 36*(1), 91-107.

Lewis, J., Arnold, M. S., House, R., & Toporek, R. (2003). *Advocacy competencies* [Electronic version]. Retrieved May 2, 2012, from http://www.counseling.org/Resources/Competencies/Advocacy_Competencies.pdf.

Martin, P. J., & House, R. M. (2002). *Transforming school counseling in the transforming school counseling initiative.* Washington, DC: The Education Trust.

Marzano, R. (2010). High expectations for all. *Educational Leadership, 68,* 82-85.

Mason, E. (2010). Leadership practices of school counselors and counseling program implementation. *NASSP Bulletin, (4).*

Mason, E. C. & McMahon, H. G. (2009). Leadership practices of school counselors. *Professional School Counseling, 13,* 107 – 115.

Myrick, R. D. (2003). *Developmental guidance and counseling: A practical approach* (4th ed.). Minneapolis, MN: Educational Media Corporation.

National School Boards Association (2009). *The key works of school boards guidebook.* Alexandria, VA: Author.

Northouse, G. (2007). *Leadership theory and practice.* (3rd ed.) Thousand Oak, London, New Delhe, Sage Publications, Inc.

Ratts, J. M., DeKruyf, L., & Chen-Hayes, S. F. (2007). The ACA advocacy competencies: A social justice advocacy framework for professional school counselors. *Professional School Counseling, 11*, 90-97.

Rowell, L. (2006). Action research and school counseling: Closing the gap between research and practice. *Professional School Counseling, 9*, 376-384.

Shillingford, M. A., and Lambie, G. W. (2010). Contribution of professional school counselors' values and leadership practices to their programmatic service delivery. *Professional School Counseling, 13*(4), 208-217.

Singleton, G. E., & Linton, C. (2006). *Courageous conversations about race.* Thousand Oaks, CA: Corwin Press.

The Council of Chief State School Officers. (2008). *Educational leadership policy standards: ISLLC 2008.* Washington, DC; Author.

The College Board, American School Counselor Association & National Association of Secondary School Principals (2009). *Finding a way: Practical examples of how an effective principal-counselor relationship can lead to success for all students.* New York: College Board.

The Education Trust, (1997). *The national guidance and counseling reform program.* Washington, DC: Author.

Therapy. 2012. In Merriam-Webster.com. Retrieved May 8, 2012 from http://www.merriam-webster.com/dictionary/therapy.

Tichy, N. M. (2004) *The cycle of leadership: How great leaders teach their companies to win.* New York: Harper Collins.

Toporek, R. L., Lewis, J. A., & Crethar, H. C. (2009). Promoting systemic change through the ACA advocacy competencies. *Journal of Counseling & Development, 87*, 260-268.

Virginia School Counselor Association (2008). *Virginia professional school counseling program manual.* Yorktown, VA: Author.

Ward, C. A. (2009). *An examination of the impact of the ASCA National Model on student achievement at recognized ASCA model program (RAMP) elementary schools.* Texas A&M University - Corpus Christi). ProQuest Dissertations and Theses, http://search.proquest.com/docview/89238070?accountid=14244

Ware, W., & Galassi, J. (2006) Using correlational and prediction data to enhance student achievement in k-12 schools: A practical application for school counselors. *Professional School Counseling, 9*, 344-356.

Whiston, S. C . & Quinby, R. F. (2009). Review of school counseling outcome research. *Psychology in the Schools, 46*(3), 267-272.

Young, A., & Kaffenberger, C. (2009). *Making data work* (2nd ed.). Alexandria, VA: American School Counselor Association.

Young, A., & Kaffenberger, C. (2011). The beliefs and practices of school counselors who use data to implement school counseling programs. *Professional School Counseling, 15*, 67-76.

Recognized ASCA Model Program (RAMP)

Drive your school counseling program to the next level. Show your administrators, school board and the community at large that you're committed to delivering a comprehensive, data-driven school counseling program. Apply for the Recognized ASCA Model Program (RAMP) designation from the American School Counselor Association.

Based on "The ASCA National Model: A Framework for School Counseling Programs," the RAMP designation:
- Gives you the confidence that your program aligns with a nationally accepted and recognized model
- Helps you evaluate your program and identify areas for improvement
- Increases your skills and knowledge of school counseling
- Enhances your program's efforts toward academic achievement and student success
- Identifies your school as an exemplary educational environment

If your program successfully answers the question, "How are students different because of what school counselors do?" then you're ready to show the world that your program is "ramped up." The RAMP application process should be the culmination of the implementation of a comprehensive school counseling program. Once your school has a program in place, you will need at least one entire academic year to collect the data and information needed to fulfill the RAMP application requirements.

For submission deadlines, an application and more information about the many benefits of achieving RAMP status, visit *www.ASCANationalModel.org*.

School Counselor Competencies

I. SCHOOL COUNSELING PROGRAMS

School counselors should possess the knowledge, abilities, skills and attitudes necessary to plan, organize, implement and evaluate a comprehensive, developmental, results-based school counseling program that aligns with the ASCA National Model.

I-A: Knowledge

ASCA's position statement, The Professional School Counselor and School Counseling Preparation Programs, states that school counselors should articulate and demonstrate an understanding of:

- ☐ I-A-1. The organizational structure and governance of the American educational system as well as cultural, political and social influences on current educational practices
- ☐ I-A-2. The organizational structure and components of an effective school counseling program that aligns with the ASCA National Model
- ☐ I-A-3. Barriers to student learning and use of advocacy and data-driven school counseling practices to close the achievement/opportunity gap
- ☐ I-A-4. Leadership principles and theories
- ☐ I-A-5. Individual counseling, group counseling and classroom instruction ensuring equitable access to resources promoting academic achievement, career development andpersonal/social development for every student
- ☐ I-A-6. Collaborations with stakeholders such as parents and guardians, teachers, administrators and community leaders to create learning environments that promote educational equity and success for every student
- ☐ I-A-7. Legal, ethical and professional issues in pre-K–12 schools
- ☐ I-A-8. Developmental theory, learning theories, social justice theory, multiculturalism, counseling theories and career counseling theories
- ☐ I-A-9. The continuum of mental health services, including prevention and intervention strategies to enhance student success

Revised, 2012

I-B: Abilities and Skills

An effective school counselor is able to accomplish measurable objectives demonstrating the following abilities and skills.

☐ I-B-1.   Plans, organizes, implements and evaluates a school counseling program aligning with the ASCA National Model

☐ I-B-1a.   Creates a vision statement examining the professional and personal competencies and qualities a school counselor should possess

☐ I-B-1b.   Describes the rationale for a comprehensive school counseling program

☐ I-B-1c.   Applies the school counseling themes of leadership, advocacy, collaboration and systemic change, which are critical to a successful school counseling program

☐ I-B-1d.   Describes, defines and identifies the qualities of an effective school counseling program

☐ I-B-1e.   Describes the benefits of a comprehensive school counseling program for all stakeholders, including students, parents, teachers, administrators, school boards, department of education, school counselors, counselor educators, community stakeholders and business leaders

☐ I-B-1f.   Describes the history of school counseling to create a context for the current state of the profession and comprehensive school counseling programs

☐ I-B-1g.   Uses technology effectively and efficiently to plan, organize, implement and evaluate the comprehensive school counseling program

☐ I-B-1h.   Demonstrates multicultural, ethical and professional competencies in planning, organizing, implementing and evaluating the comprehensive school counseling program

☐ I-B-2.   Serves as a leader in the school and community to promote and support student success

☐ I-B-2a.   Understands and defines leadership and its role in comprehensive school counseling programs

☐ I-B-2b.   Identifies and applies a model of leadership to a comprehensive school counseling program

☐ I-B-2c.   Identifies and demonstrates professional and personal qualities and skills of effective leaders

☐ I-B-2d.   Identifies and applies components of the ASCA National Model requiring leadership, such as an advisory council, management tools and accountability

☐ I-B-2e.   Creates a plan to challenge the non-counseling tasks that are assigned to school counselors

☐ I-B-3.   Advocates for student success

☐ I-B-3a.   Understands and defines advocacy and its role in comprehensive school counseling programs

☐ I-B-3b.   Identifies and demonstrates benefits of advocacy with school and community stakeholders

☐ I-B-3c.   Describes school counselor advocacy competencies, which include dispositions, knowledge and skills

☐ I-B-3d.   Reviews advocacy models and develops a personal advocacy plan

☐ I-B-3e.   Understands the process for development of policy and procedures at the build-
            ing, district, state and national levels

☐ I-B-4.   Collaborates with parents, teachers, administrators, community leaders and
            other stakeholders to promote and support student success
☐ I-B-4a.   Defines collaboration and its role in comprehensive school counseling pro-
            grams
☐ I-B-4b.   Identifies and applies models of collaboration for effective use in a school
            counseling program and understands the similarities and differences between
            consultation, collaboration and counseling and coordination strategies
☐ I-B-4c.   Creates statements or other documents delineating the various roles of student
            service providers, such as school social worker, school psychologist or school
            nurse, and identifies best practices for collaborating to affect student success
☐ I-B-4d.   Understands and knows how to apply a consensus-building process to foster
            agreement in a group
☐ I-B-4e.   Understands how to facilitate group meetings to effectively and efficiently meet
            group goals

☐ I-B-5.   Acts as a systems change agent to create an environment promoting and sup-
            porting student success
☐ I-B-5a.   Defines and understands system change and its role in comprehensive school
            counseling programs
☐ I-B-5b.   Develops a plan to deal with personal (emotional and cognitive) and institu-
            tional resistance impeding the change process
☐ I-B-5c.   Understands the impact of school, district and state educational policies, proce-
            dures and practices supporting and/or impeding student success

I-C: Attitudes
School counselors believe:
☐ I-C-1.   Every student can learn, and every student can succeed
☐ I-C-2.   Every student should have access to and opportunity for a high-quality educa-
            tion
☐ I-C-3.   Every student should graduate from high school and be prepared for employ-
            ment or college and other post-secondary education
☐ I-C-4.   Every student should have access to a school counseling program
☐ I-C-5.   Effective school counseling is a collaborative process involving school coun-
            selors, students, parents, teachers, administrators, community leaders and
            other stakeholders
☐ I-C-6.   School counselors can and should be leaders in the school and district
☐ I-C-7.   The effectiveness of school counseling programs should be measurable using
            process, perception and outcome data

II: FOUNDATIONS

School counselors should possess the knowledge, abilities, skills and attitudes necessary to establish the foundations of a school counseling program aligning with the ASCA National Model.

II-A: Knowledge
School counselors should articulate and demonstrate an understanding of:
- [ ] II-A-1. Beliefs and vision of the school counseling program that align with current school improvement and student success initiatives at the school, district and state level
- [ ] II-A-2. Educational systems, philosophies and theories and current trends in education, including federal and state legislation
- [ ] II-A-3. Learning theories
- [ ] II-A-4. History and purpose of school counseling, including traditional and transformed roles of school counselors
- [ ] II-A-5. Human development theories and developmental issues affecting student success
- [ ] II-A-6. District, state and national student standards and competencies, including ASCA Student Standards and other student standards that may complement and inform the comprehensive school counseling program
- [ ] II-A-7. Legal and ethical standards and principles of the school counseling profession and educational systems, including district and building policies
- [ ] II-A-8. The three domains of academic achievement, career planning and personal/social development

II-B: Abilities and Skills
An effective school counselor is able to accomplish measurable objectives demonstrating the following abilities and skills:
- [ ] II-B-1. Develops the beliefs and vision of the school counseling program that align with current school improvement and student success initiatives at the school, district and state level
- [ ] II-B-1a. Examines personal, district and state beliefs, assumptions and philosophies about student success, specifically what they should know and be able to do
- [ ] II-B-1b. Demonstrates knowledge of a school's particular educational vision and mission
- [ ] II-B-1c. Conceptualizes and writes a personal philosophy about students, families, teachers, school counseling programs and the educational process consistent with the school's educational philosophy and mission
- [ ] II-B-1d. Writes a school counseling vision statement that describes a future world in which the school counseling goals and strategies are being successfully achieved

- [ ] II-B-2. Develops a school counseling mission statement aligning with the school, district and state mission
- [ ] II-B-2a. Critiques a school district mission statement and identifies or writes a mission statement aligning with beliefs

☐ II-B-2b. Writes a school counseling mission statement that is specific, concise, clear and comprehensive, describing a school counseling program's purpose and a vision of the program's benefits for every student

☐ II-B-2c. Communicates the vision and mission of the school counseling program to all appropriate stakeholders

☐ II-B-3. Uses student standards, such as ASCA Student Standards and other appropriate student standards such as district or state standards, to drive the implementation of a comprehensive school counseling program

☐ II-B-3a. Crosswalks the ASCA Student Standards with other appropriate student standards

☐ II-B-3b. Prioritizes student standards that align with the school's goals

☐ II-B-4. Applies the ethical standards and principles of the school counseling profession and adheres to the legal aspects of the role of the school counselor

☐ II-B-4a. Practices ethical principles of the school counseling profession in accordance with the ASCA Ethical Standards for School Counselors

☐ II-B-4b. Understands the legal and ethical nature of working in a pluralistic, multicultural and technological society

☐ II-B-4c. Understands and practices in accordance with school district policy and local, state and federal statutory requirements

☐ II-B-4d. Understands the unique legal and ethical nature of working with minor students in a school setting

☐ II-B-4e. Advocates responsibly for school board policy and local, state and federal statutory requirements in students' best interests

☐ II-B-4f. Resolves ethical dilemmas by employing an ethical decision-making model appropriate to work in schools

☐ II-B-4g. Models ethical behavior

☐ II-B-4h. Continuously engages in professional development and uses resources to inform and guide ethical and legal work

☐ II-B-4i. Practices within the ethical and statutory limits of confidentiality

☐ II-B-4j. Continually seeks consultation and supervision to guide legal and ethical decision making and to recognize and resolve ethical dilemmas

☐ II-B-4k. Understands and applies an ethical and legal obligation not only to students but to parents, administration and teachers as well

II-C: Attitudes

School counselors demonstrate their attitudes and beliefs that all students deserve access to a comprehensive program that:

☐ II-C-1. Has an impact on every student rather than a series of services provided only to students in need

☐ II-C-2. Is an integral component of student success and the overall mission of the school and school district

☐ II-C-3. Promotes and supports academic achievement, career planning and personal/social development for every student

☐ II-C-4. Adheres to school and district policies, state laws and regulations and professional ethics standards

☐ II-C-5. Is intentional in addressing the information, opportunity and achievement gaps

III: MANAGEMENT

School counselors should possess the knowledge, abilities, skills and attitudes necessary to manage a school counseling program aligning with the ASCA National Model.

III-A: Knowledge
School counselors should articulate and demonstrate an understanding of:
☐ III-A-1. Leadership principles, including sources of power and authority and formal and informal leadership
☐ III-A-2. Organization theory to facilitate advocacy, collaboration and systemic change
☐ III-A-3. Presentation skills for programs such as teacher in-services, parent workshops and presentation of results reports to school boards
☐ III-A-4. Time management, including long- and short-term management using tools such as schedules and calendars
☐ III-A-5. Data-driven decision making
☐ III-A-6. Current and emerging technologies such as use of the Internet, Web-based resources and information management systems

III-B: Abilities and Skills
An effective school counselor is able to accomplish measurable objectives demonstrating the following abilities and skills:

☐ III-B-1. Self-evaluates his/her own competencies leading to and resulting in the formulation of an appropriate professional development plan
☐ III-B-1a. Conducts a school counseling program assessment
☐ III-B-1b. Negotiates a management plan for the comprehensive school counseling program with the administrator
☐ III-B-1c. Discusses and develops the management component of the school counseling program with the other members of the school counseling staff
☐ III-B-1d. Presents school counseling management tools to the principal, and finalizes an annual school counseling agreement
☐ III-B-1e. Discusses the anticipated program results when implementing the action plans for the school year
☐ III-B-1f. Participates in school counseling and education-related professional organizations
☐ III-B-1g. Develops a yearly professional development plan demonstrating how the school counselor advances relevant knowledge, skills and dispositions
☐ III-B-1h. Communicates effective goals and benchmarks for meeting and exceeding expectations consistent with the administrator/school counselor annual agreement and district performance appraisals
☐ III-B-1i. Uses personal reflection, consultation and supervision to promote professional growth and development

☐ III-B-2. Establishes and convenes an advisory council for the comprehensive school counseling program

☐ III-B-2a. Uses leadership skills to facilitate vision and positive change for the comprehensive school counseling program

☐ III-B-2b. Determines appropriate education stakeholders who should be represented on the advisory council

☐ III-B-2c. Develops effective and efficient meeting agendas

☐ III-B-2d. Reviews school data, school counseling program assessment and school counseling program goals with the advisory council

☐ III-B-2e. Records meeting notes and distributes as appropriate

☐ III-B-2f. Analyzes and incorporates feedback from the advisory council related to school counseling program goals as appropriate

☐ III-B-3. Accesses or collects relevant data, including process, perception and outcome data, to monitor and improve student behavior and achievement

☐ III-B-3a. Reviews and disaggregates student achievement, attendance and behavior data to identify and implement interventions as needed

☐ III-B-3b. Uses data to identify policies, practices and procedures leading to successes, systemic barriers and areas of weakness

☐ III-B-3c. Uses student data to demonstrate a need for systemic change in areas such as course enrollment patterns; equity and access; and achievement, opportunity and/or information gaps

☐ III-B-3d. Understands and uses data to establish goals and activities to close the achievement, opportunity and/or information gap

☐ III-B-3e. Knows how to use data to identify gaps between and among different groups of students

☐ III-B-3f. Uses school data to identify and assist individual students who do not perform at grade level and do not have opportunities and resources to be successful in school

☐ III-B-3g. Knows and understands theoretical and historical basis for assessment techniques

☐ III-B-4. Assesses use of time in direct and indirect student services and program management and school support

☐ III-B-4a. Organizes and manages time to effectively implement a comprehensive school counseling program

☐ III-B-4b. Identifies appropriate distribution of school counselor's time based on the school data and program goals

☐ III-B-4c. Creates a rationale for school counselor's use of time in the delivery component to focus on the goals of the comprehensive school counseling program

☐ III-B-4d. Identifies and evaluates fair-share responsibilities, which articulate appropriate and inappropriate counseling and non-counseling activities

☐ III-B-5. Develops calendars to ensure the effective implementation of the school counseling program

☐ III-B-5a. Creates annual and weekly calendars to plan activities to reflect school counseling program goals

☐ III-B-5b. Demonstrates time-management skills including scheduling, publicizing and prioritizing time and tasks

☐ III-B-6. Designs and implements action plans aligning with school and school counseling program goals

☐ III-B-6a. Uses appropriate academic and behavioral data to develop school counseling core curriculum, small-group and closing-the-gap action plans and determines appropriate students for the target group or interventions

☐ III-B-6b. Identifies ASCA domains, standards and competencies being addressed by each plan

☐ III-B-6c. Creates lesson plans related to the school counseling core curriculum identifying what will be delivered, to whom it will be delivered, how it will be delivered and how student attainment of competencies will be evaluated

☐ III-B-6d. Determines the intended impact on academics, attendance and behavior

☐ III-B-6e. Identifies appropriate activities to accomplish objectives

☐ III-B-6f. Identifies appropriate resources needed

☐ III-B-6g. Identifies data-collection strategies to gather process, perception and outcome data

☐ III-B-6h. Shares results of action plans with staff, parents and community.

☐ III-B-7. Implements program management and school support activities for the comprehensive school counseling program

☐ III-B-7a. Creates a program management and school support planning document addressing school counselor's responsibilities for program management and professional development

☐ III-B-7b. Coordinates activities that establish, maintain and enhance the school counseling program as well as other educational programs

☐ III-B-8. Conducts self-appraisal related to school counseling skills and performance

III-C: Attitudes

School counselors believe:

☐ III-C-1. A school counseling program/department must be managed like other programs and departments in a school

☐ III-C-2. Planning, organizing, implementing and evaluating a school counseling program are critical responsibilities for a school counselor

☐ III-C-3. Management of a school counseling program must be done in collaboration with administrators

IV: DELIVERY

School counselors should possess the knowledge, abilities, skills and attitudes necessary to deliver a school counseling program aligning with the ASCA National Model.

IV-A: Knowledge
School counselors should articulate and demonstrate an understanding of:
- ☐ IV-A-1. The distinction between direct and indirect student services
- ☐ IV-A-2. The concept of a school counseling core curriculum
- ☐ IV-A-3. Counseling theories and techniques that work in school, such as rational emotive behavior therapy, reality therapy, cognitive-behavioral therapy, Alderian, solution-focused brief counseling, person-centered counseling and family systems
- ☐ IV-A-4. Counseling theories and techniques in different settings, such as individual planning, group counseling and classroom lessons
- ☐ IV-A-5. Classroom management
- ☐ IV-A-6. Principles of career planning and college admissions, including financial aid and athletic eligibility
- ☐ IV-A-7. Principles of working with various student populations based on characteristics such as ethnic and racial background, English language proficiency, special needs, religion, gender and income
- ☐ IV-A-8. Principles of multi-tiered approaches within the context of a comprehensive school counseling program
- ☐ IV-A-9. Responsive services (counseling and crisis response) including grief and bereavement
- ☐ IV-A-10. The differences between counseling, collaboration and consultation, especially the potential for dual roles with parents, guardians and other caretakers

IV-B: Abilities and Skills
An effective school counselor is able to accomplish measurable objectives demonstrating the following abilities and skills.

Direct Student Services
School Counseling Core Curriculum
- ☐ IV-B-1. Implements the school counseling core curriculum
- ☐ IV-B-1a. Identifies appropriate curriculum aligned to ASCA Student Standards
- ☐ IV-B-1b. Develops and presents a developmental school counseling core curriculum addressing all students' needs based on student data
- ☐ IV-B-1c. Demonstrates classroom management and instructional skills
- ☐ IV-B-1d. Develops materials and instructional strategies to meet student needs and school goals
- ☐ IV-B-1e. Encourages staff involvement to ensure the effective implementation of the school counseling core curriculum
- ☐ IV-B-1f. Knows, understands and uses a variety of technology in the delivery of school counseling core curriculum activities

☐ IV-B-1g. Understands multicultural and pluralistic trends when developing and choosing school counseling core curriculum

☐ IV-B-1h. Understands and is able to build effective, high-quality peer helper programs

Individual Student Planning

☐ IV-B-2. Facilitates individual student planning

☐ IV-B-2a. Understands individual student planning as a component of a comprehensive program

☐ IV-B-2b. Develops strategies to implement individual student planning, such as strategies for appraisal, advisement, goal-setting, decision-making, social skills, transition or post-secondary planning

☐ IV-B-2c. Helps students establish goals and develops and uses planning skills in collaboration with parents or guardians and school personnel

☐ IV-B-2d. Understands career opportunities, labor market trends and global economics and uses various career assessment techniques to help students understand their abilities and career interests

☐ IV-B-2e. Helps students learn the importance of college and other post-secondary education and helps students navigate the college admissions process

☐ IV-B-2f. Understands the relationship of academic performance to the world of work, family life and community service

☐ IV-B-2g. Understands methods for helping students monitor and direct their own learning and personal/social and career development

Responsive Services

☐ IV-B-3. Provides responsive services

☐ IV-B-3a. Lists and describes interventions used in responsive services, such as individual/small-group counseling and crisis response

☐ IV-B-3b. Understands appropriate individual and small-group counseling theories and techniques such as rational emotive behavior therapy, reality therapy, cognitive-behavioral therapy, Adlerian, solution-focused brief counseling, person-centered counseling and family systems

☐ IV-B-3c. Demonstrates an ability to provide counseling for students during times of transition, separation, heightened stress and critical change

☐ IV-B-3d. Understands what defines a crisis, the appropriate response and a variety of intervention strategies to meet the needs of the individual, group or school community before, during and after crisis response

☐ IV-B-3e. Provides team leadership to the school and community in a crisis

☐ IV-B-3f. Involves appropriate school and community professionals as well as the family in a crisis situation

☐ IV-B-3g. Understands the nature of academic, career and personal/social counseling in schools and the similarities and differences among school counseling and other types of counseling, such as mental health, marriage and family and substance abuse counseling, within a continuum of care

☐ IV-B-3h. Understands the role of the school counselor and the school counseling program in the school crisis plan

Indirect Student Services
Referrals
☐ IV-B-4a. Understands how to make referrals to appropriate professionals when necessary
☐ IV-B-4b. Compiles referral resources to utilize with students, staff and families to effectively address issues
☐ IV-B-4c. Develops a list of community agencies and service providers for student referrals

Consultation
☐ IV-B-5a. Shares strategies that support student achievement with parents, teachers, other educators and community organizations
☐ IV-B-5b. Applies appropriate counseling approaches to promoting change among consultees within a consultation approach
☐ IV-B-5c. Works with education stakeholders to better understand student needs and to identify strategies that promote student achievement

Collaboration
☐ IV-B-6a. Partners with parents, teachers, administrators and education stakeholders for student achievement and success
☐ IV-B-6b. Conducts in-service training or workshops for other stakeholders to share school counseling expertise
☐ IV-B-6c. Understands and knows how to provide supervision for school counseling interns consistent with the principles of the ASCA National Model

IV-C: Attitudes
School counselors believe:
☐ IV-C-1. School counseling is one component in the continuum of care that should be available to all students
☐ IV-C-2. School counselors coordinate and facilitate counseling and other services to ensure all students receive the care they need, even though school counselors may not personally provide the care themselves
☐ IV-C-3. School counselors engage in developmental counseling and short-term responsive counseling
☐ IV-C-4. School counselors should refer students to district or community resources to meet more extensive needs such as long-term therapy or diagnoses of disorders

V: ACCOUNTABILITY

School counselors should possess the knowledge, abilities, skills and attitudes necessary to monitor and evaluate the processes and results of a school counseling program aligning with the ASCA National Model.

V-A: Knowledge

School counselors should articulate and demonstrate an understanding of:

☐ V-A-1. Basic concepts of results-based school counseling and accountability issues
☐ V-A-2. Basic research sampling, methodology and analysis concepts to understand research outcomes and conduct action research
☐ V-A-3. Use of data to evaluate program effectiveness and to determine program needs
☐ V-A-4. School counseling program assessments and results reports

V-B: Abilities and Skills

An effective school counselor is able to accomplish measurable objectives demonstrating the following abilities and skills.

☐ V-B-1. Analyzes data from school data profile and results reports to evaluate student outcomes and program effectiveness and to determine program needs
☐ V-B-1a. Analyzes use of time to determine how much time is spent in school counseling program components and considers best use of time compared to student needs as identified through student data
☐ V-B-1b. Analyzes results from school counseling program assessment
☐ V-B-1c. Uses formal and informal methods of program evaluation to design and enhance comprehensive school counseling programs
☐ V-B-1d. Uses student data to support decision-making in designing effective school counseling programs and interventions
☐ V-B-1e. Measures and analyzes results attained from school counseling core curriculum, small group and closing-the-gap activities
☐ V-B-1f. Works with members of the school counseling team and with the administration to decide how school counseling programs are evaluated and how results are shared
☐ V-B-1g. Analyzes and interprets process, perception and outcome data
☐ V-B-1h. Reviews progress toward program goals

☐ V-B-1i. Uses technology in conducting research and program evaluation
☐ V-B-1j. Reports program results to the school counseling community
☐ V-B-1k. Uses data to demonstrate the value the school counseling program adds to student achievement
☐ V-B-1l. Uses results obtained for program improvement

☐ V-B-2. Understands and advocates for appropriate school counselor performance appraisal process based on school counselor competencies and implementation of the comprehensive school counseling program
☐ V-B-2a. Analyzes self-assessment related to school counseling skills and performance
☐ V-B-2b. Identifies how school counseling activities fit within categories of a performance appraisal instrument
☐ V-B-2c. Encourages administrators to use a performance appraisal instrument reflecting appropriate responsibilities for school counselors

- [ ] V-B-3a. Compares current school counseling program implementation with the ASCA National Model
- [ ] V-B-3b. Shares the results of the program assessment with administrators, the advisory council and other appropriate stakeholders
- [ ] V-B-3c. Identifies areas for improvement for the school counseling program

V-C: Attitudes

School counselors believe:

- [ ] V-C-1. School counseling programs should achieve demonstrable results
- [ ] V-C-2. School counselors should be accountable for the results of the school counseling program
- [ ] V-C-3. School counselors should use quantitative and qualitative data to evaluate their school counseling program and to demonstrate program results
- [ ] V-C-4. The outcomes of the school counseling program should be analyzed and presented in the context of the overall school and district performance

Acknowledgements

The ASCA National Model is a compilation of theory, practices, documents and writings from leaders in the field of school counseling. Many school counseling books and materials were used in the creation of the document. ASCA would like to extend its sincere appreciation to the authors of the following documents who graciously contributed their work as the principle influences in the creation of the first edition of "The ASCA National Model: A Foundation for School Counseling Programs."

Gysbers, N. C. & Henderson, P. (2000). *Developing and managing your school guidance program* (3rd ed). Alexandria, VA: American Counseling Association.

Johnson, C. D. & Johnson, S. K. (1997). *Results-based student support programs*. San Juan Capistrano, CA: Professional Update.

Myrick, R.D. (2003). *Developmental guidance and counseling: A practical approach*. (4th ed). Minneapolis, MN: Education Media Corporation.

ASCA extends its sincere appreciation to the authors of the original edition, Judy Bowers, Ed.D., and Trish Hatch, Ph.D. ASCA also extends its sincere appreciation to the authors of the following works, which influenced the creation and revisions of the ASCA National Model to varying degrees and have been infused throughout the document.

Arizona Department of Education (2002). *Arizona counselor academy program handbook*. Tucson, AZ: Center for Educational Development.

Bowers, J. L. & Colonna, H. A. (2001). *Tucson Unified School District guidance and counseling program handbook*. Tucson, AZ: Tucson Unified School District.

Campbell, C. A. & Dahir, C. A. (1997). *Sharing the vision: The national standards for school counseling programs*. Alexandra, VA: American School Counselor Association Press.

Dahir, C. A., Sheldon, C. B. & Valiga, M. J. (1998). *Vision into action: Implementing the national standards for school counseling programs*. Alexandria, VA: American School Counselor Association Press.

Dimmitt, C., Carey, J. C., and Hatch, T. (2007). *Evidence-based school counseling: Making a difference with data-driven practices*. Thousand Oaks, CA: Corwin Press.

Gysbers, N. C. & Henderson, P. (2012). *Developing and managing your school guidance program* (5th ed.). Alexandria, VA: American Counseling Association.

Hatch, T. & Holland, L.A. (2001). *Moreno Valley Unified District school counselor academy handbook*. Moreno Valley, CA: Moreno Valley Unified School District.

Henderson, P. & Gysbers, C. N. (1998). *Leading and managing your school guidance staff*. Alexandra, VA: American Counseling Association.

Johnson, C. D. & Johnson, S. K. (2001). *Results-based student support programs: Leadership academy workbook*. San Juan Capistrano, CA: Professional Update.

Martin, P. J. & House, R. M. (2002). *Transforming school counseling in the transforming school counseling initiative*. Washington, DC: The Education Trust.

The Education Trust (2002). *National school counselor initiative: Met Life Foundation*. Washington, DC: Author.

Virginia School Counseling Association (2008). *Virginia professional school counseling program manual*. Yorktown, VA: Author.

Young, A., & Kaffenberger, C. (2009). *Making data work* (2nd ed.). Alexandria, VA: American School Counselor Association.

ASCA wishes to thank the following school counselors, district directors and school counselor educators who served on the ASCA National Model (third edition) Advisory Committee.

Judy Bowers, Ed.D., Retired Coordinator of the School Counseling Program, Tucson Unified School District, Ariz.

Jill Cook, ASCA Assistant Director

Vanessa Gomez-Lee, School Counselor, Valley View High School, Moreno Valley, Calif.

Norm Gysbers, Ph.D., Curators' Professor, University of Missouri – Columbia

Trish Hatch, Ph.D., Associate Professor, San Diego State University

Carol Kaffenberger, Ph.D., Associate Professor Emerita, George Mason University

Mark Kuranz, ASCA Director of Professional Development

Michelle James, School Counselor, General Smallwood Middle School, Indian Head, Md.

Anthony Pearson, School Counselor, Sky View Elementary School, Mableton, Ga.

Marrius Pettiford, Ph.D., Director of Student Support Services, Alamance-Burlington School System, N.C.

Kathleen Rakestraw, ASCA Director of Communications

Christopher Sink, Ph.D., Professor, Seattle Pacific University

Eric Sparks, Ed.D., ASCA Assistant Director

Kwok-Sze Wong, Ed.D., ASCA Executive Director